Welcome to the *EVERYTHING®* series!

THESE HANDY, accessible books give you all you need to tackle a difficult project, gain a new hobby, comprehend a fascinating topic, prepare for an exam, or even brush up on something you learned back in school but have since forgotten.

You can read an *EVERYTHING®* book from cover-to-cover or just pick out the information you want from our four useful boxes: e-facts, e-ssentials, e-alerts, and e-questions. We literally give you everything you need to know on the subject, but throw in a lot of fun stuff along the way, too.

We now have well over 150 *EVERYTHING®* books in print, spanning such wide-ranging topics as weddings, pregnancy, wine, learning guitar, one-pot cooking, managing people, and so much more. When you're done reading them all, you can finally say you know *EVERYTHING®*!

 **FACTS:** Important sound bytes of information

 **ESSENTIALS:** Quick and handy tips

 **ALERTS!:** Urgent warnings

 **QUESTIONS:** Solutions to common problems

THE

EVERYTHING® Series

Dear Reader,

I've had the privilege of attending, observing, and participating in many weddings. Which means I've also been a bridesmaid multiple times, for better or worse. In that interim I also planned my own wedding, which offered up some valuable insight into the other side. And the ultimate conclusion I've come to about bridesmaids is this: It's all about the bride, and not at all about the maids. The best bridesmaid is completely selfless, willing to work silently behind the scenes, and eager to lend a hand . . . without getting carried away. She's there strictly to make the bride's wedding day—and the days preceding it—even better for her. Knowing this doesn't necessarily make it easy, of course.

And that's why I've written this book. Because the role of the bridesmaid is not etched in stone, this book is meant to serve as a starting point and guide for reaching your ultimate goal—helping to create bridal bliss. So good luck and more important, have fun!

THE EVERYTHING® BRIDESMAID BOOK

From planning the shower to supporting the bride—all you need to survive and enjoy the wedding

Jennifer Lata Rung

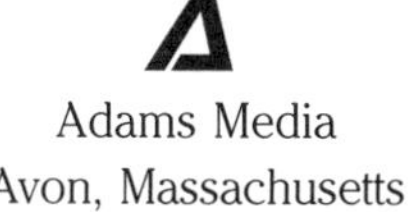

Adams Media
Avon, Massachusetts

To my sister Kim—a beautiful bridesmaid, inside & out

An Everything® Series Book.
Everything® is a registered trademark of F+W Publications, Inc.

Published by Adams Media, an F+W Publications Company
57 Littlefield Street, Avon, MA 02322 U.S.A.
www.adamsmedia.com

ISBN: 1-58062-982-2
Printed in Canada.

J I H G F E D C

Library of Congress Cataloging-in-Publication Data
Rung, Jennifer Lata.
The everything bridesmaid book / Jennifer Lata Rung.
p. cm.
(An everything series book)
ISBN 1-58062-982-2
1. Bridesmaids. 2. Wedding etiquette. I. Title. II. Series:
Everything series.
BJ2065.W43R86 2004
395.2'2–dc22 2003016973

Illustrations by Barry Littmann.

THE

EVERYTHING®

Series

EDITORIAL

Publishing Director: Gary M. Krebs
Managing Editor: Kate McBride
Copy Chief: Laura MacLaughlin
Acquisitions Editor: Bethany Brown
Development Editor: Karen Jacot Johnson
Production Editor: Khrysti Nazzaro,
Jamie Wielgus

PRODUCTION

Production Director: Susan Beale
Production Manager: Michelle Roy Kelly
Series Designer: Daria Perreault
Cover Design: Paul Beatrice and Frank Rivera
Layout and Graphics: Colleen Cunningham,
Rachael Eiben, Michelle Roy Kelly,
Daria Perreault, Erin Ring

Contents

Acknowledgments

Thanks to the beautiful brides with whom I "researched" this book over the years–Tammy, Jen, Nina, Deena, Kate, Emily, and Miffy. And thanks to my own maids for making it all so much fun.

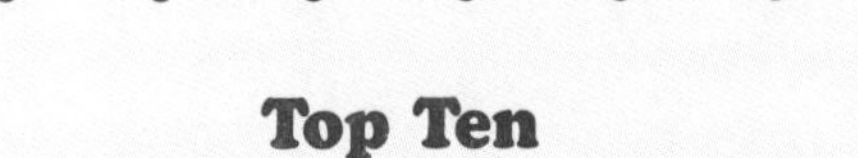

Top Ten
Bridesmaid Controversies

1. You weren't asked.
2. You were asked—but you're not sure why.
3. She asked you—but you're not planning on asking *her*.
4. Her metamorphosis into Bridezilla is complete.
5. You blow off your bridesmaid duties.
6. You're not crazy about the other bridesmaids.
7. The other bridesmaids could care less about you.
8. You love the bride—but can't tolerate the groom.
9. She's all about the Vera Wang—and you're on a Goodwill budget.
10. The dress lives up to the cliché.

Introduction

THERE'S NO ARGUING: It's her day. So where does that leave you? Playing understudy to her bright shining star? Benchwarmer to her starting position? Ugly stepsister to her Cinderella? Well, yes. And no. We both know you're no ugly stepsister. But we also know that as a bridesmaid, you're not the intended recipient of the coveted glass slipper (or the platinum-set diamond). If you're used to being the center of attention, adopting this role may take some time and patience, but remember, your time will come, if it hasn't already. Keep in mind, however, that there will be plenty of behind-the-scenes responsibilities that will, from time to time, serve to shed light on your existence. With that in mind, it's important to be prepared when that fleeting glare falls temporarily on you.

You've probably already heard tell of some of your supposed responsibilities, like throwing a shower, hosting a bachelorette party, plus helping the bride in a myriad of other ways—most of which seem a bit nebulous and difficult to pin down. Your mother's telling you one thing, the bride's telling you another, and your cousin is telling you something altogether different. Who's right? And to whom should you ultimately listen?

The Everything® Bridesmaid Book takes the mystery out of the prewedding mayhem—and provides you with options that you and your fellow bridesmaids will feel comfortable following, from the shower to the bridesmaid dress to the bachelorette party and beyond.

So relax, read on, and most important, have some fun. Be the off-center of attention. And see how rewarding the supporting role can actually be.

Chapter 1

So You've Been Asked to Be a Bridesmaid

Your best friend is getting married. Or maybe it's your sister, your childhood chum, or distant cousin. No matter. She's asked you to be a bridesmaid, and you've said yes. Now you want to know, what's next? And what, exactly, does being a bridesmaid mean today? Read on to find out what this honor entails and what might be expected of you, and, most important, whether you'll have to wear pink taffeta.

An Honored Post

First of all, consider it a real honor that you've been asked to be a bridesmaid. After all, the implication is that someone likes you enough to desire your close participation in one of the most important days of her life. Of course, that doesn't necessarily mean you like *her* enough to be part of one of the most important days of her life. This brings us back to the question: What does being a bridesmaid mean today? And what sort of commitment is required to play this role to its end?

This chapter will give a little historical perspective—in addition to some modern-day wisdom—so you can take on the role of bridesmaid with knowledge and understanding. Or, after some introspection, you may simply decide it's not for you. Either way, you'll be entering this adventure with your eyes wide open, armed with the information you need to make the right decisions every step of the way.

History of Bridesmaids

There is conflicting evidence about the role of the first bridesmaids. One legend has it that in early Roman times, the bride would be accompanied by her bridesmaids as a kind of "human shield" when traveling to the groom's village. The bridesmaids were meant to protect her from vengeful former suitors or thieves attempting to steal her dowry.

The more commonly accepted origin of the bridesmaid, however, stems from superstitions held in later

Roman times. In order to prevent the bride from being overtaken by evil spirits, up to ten bridesmaids—dressed almost identically to the bride—would accompany her during the wedding proceedings. This strategy was devised to outsmart the evil spirits believed to be present at wedding ceremonies.

FACT

Even though it began long ago, the superstition of evil spirits held its ground until as late as nineteenth-century England. If you look at some Victorian-age wedding photographs, in fact, you'd be hard-pressed to differentiate the bride from her bridesmaids.

Though the reasons have changed, the tradition has stuck. And though bridesmaids are no longer virtual twins of the bride, they are still, more often than not, twins of each other. This is most likely the result of the traditional pageantry surrounding weddings, along with the perpetuity of tradition. Of course, in recent years, more and more brides have chosen to forgo this tradition, allowing their bridesmaids to express some individuality by choosing their own color schemes or outfits. We'll talk more about these enlightened brides in Chapter 3.

Modern Bridesmaids

While bridesmaids no longer perform the function of ruses for evil spirits, or act as bodyguards against wayward thugs and thieves, they still do serve many practical functions as the bride counts down the days to her wedding. And while the duties of bridesmaid may often appear to the casual observer as nothing more than looking good for the big day, there is, in fact, much more to it . . . if the bride so desires.

In fact, there are some brides who desire nothing more than to have their bridesmaids show up in their dictated attire with hair, nails, and makeup looking perfect; these brides have an army of other helpers, such as the wedding coordinator, mother, or aunts, handling the shower, prewedding details, and anything else wedding-related. However, there are other brides who will need you desperately during the wedding planning, for tasks ranging well beyond the traditional bridesmaid duties. Warning: Both these extremes can prove tricky.

For the first scenario presented here–bridesmaid-as-figurehead–you'll be expected to do little besides show up. But at the same time, you'll need to tread carefully to avoid stepping on anyone's wedding-coordination toes. For the bridesmaid-as-indentured-servant scenario, in which you'll be expected to perform tasks well beyond the traditionally expected (such as sabotaging the bachelor party, or taking out a home equity loan to throw an elaborate shower), you'll need to learn how to say "no." With any luck, your experience will fall somewhere in between the two. Want to predict which end of the spectrum your role will fall on?

FACT

For some weddings, you may be heavily involved in wedding planning, errand running, and other duties; for others, your responsibilities will be strictly by the book. It ultimately depends on your bride's personality and style.

What's the Bride's Style?

There are subtle little prewedding predictors that can help you determine just what your bridesmaid experience will really be like. Generally, the personality and expectations of the bride will dictate this experience. Answer the following questions and consult the key at the end for some clues about what you're in for in the months that lie ahead.

1. When she's thrown parties in the past, the bride:

   a. Refuses to allow you to bring anything.
   b. Tells you to bring a bottle of wine or a small hors d'oeuvre, but only after you've harangued her relentlessly.
   c. Prefers B.Y.O. style, calling everyone who's invited to dictate what to bring, from the entrée to the cocktail mixers to dessert.

2. Which best defines the bride?

a. She's in almost daily contact with her manicurist, cleaning lady, accountant, and personal shopper.
b. She shops only with a sister or good friend, in order to get their valued opinions.
c. For her, shopping means raiding *your* closet–and frequently not returning what she's borrowed.

3. When in crisis, the bride calls:

a. Her mother.
b. Her sister or a good friend.
c. Anyone who'll listen.

4. How would you best describe your relationship with the bride?

a. Respectful, but a tad distant.
b. Equal and mutually rewarding.
c. You are her de facto therapist.

5. How does the bride envision her wedding?

a. However her mother envisions it.
b. As a starting point and celebration for a strong marriage.
c. Absolutely perfect, or you fear she'll have a breakdown.

Interpreting your answers: If your answers were mostly "A," it's a safe bet that you and the other bridesmaids will not have a great deal of prewedding responsibility. More than likely the bride will already have legions of paid helpers at her fingertips. . .or her mother to run the show. The best way to handle this situation is to ask before you plan. Check with the bride, her mother, her wedding coordinator, and any other involved parties before planning showers or other prewedding get-togethers.

If your answers were mostly "B," you'll probably have a fairly typical bridesmaid experience, and traditional etiquette will be your guide. Expect to be involved in planning a shower or bachelorette party, as well as in other prewedding duties as requested. Most likely the "B"-type bride will be reasonable in her requests and will understand that your world doesn't completely revolve around her wedding.

QUESTION?

May I say no?

It is an honor to be asked to serve as a bridesmaid, so seriously consider the pros and cons of declining before doing so. See "Excuses, Excuses," later in this chapter, to determine whether your reasons are suitable or just selfish.

If your answers were mostly "C," brace yourself. This bride needs a lot of attention and hand-holding from everyone around her. You may be at the receiving end of requests that go beyond the typical call of duty, such as scouting out vendors and caterers, running endless errands, and providing heavy-duty emotional support. All, of course, are the mark of a good friendship under normal circumstances, but beware of the bride who goes a bit too far with her demands or requests. If you're not sure as you go along, this book will help you determine which requests are reasonable—and which border on outrageous.

Bridesmaid Duties

So what are these traditional bridesmaid duties, anyway? And what is actually expected of the "typical" bridesmaid? As we just touched upon, every bride is different—and so is every wedding. That means that every bridesmaid experience will probably be different, too. However, there are some basic commonalities that characterize the role of most bridesmaids.

The "typical" bridesmaid will do the following:

- Help shop for and purchase bridesmaid attire, including dress, shoes, and accessories. This attire is usually chosen by the bride, who may or may not accept the input of bridesmaids.
- Help plan, host, and pay for a bridal shower.

- Attend all prewedding parties, including engagement parties, bridal showers, and the bridesmaids' luncheon or tea.
- Help plan and throw a bachelorette party.
- Provide help with prewedding and wedding day errands, as requested (and within reason).
- Precede the bride as she walks down the aisle.
- Be part of the post-wedding receiving line, if requested.
- Do general light hosting and helping at the wedding reception, where needed.
- Provide moral and emotional support for the bride throughout the wedding planning process and on the wedding day itself.
- Purchase a wedding gift for the bride and groom.

QUESTION?

What's the difference between a bridesmaid and a maid of honor?

The maid of honor generally has more responsibility than the bridesmaids, serving as the leader or organizer of the bridal party and their duties. (See Chapter 2 for more.)

Again, your experience as a bridesmaid will differ, depending upon the bride and her disposition. Some brides may call you to help run errands on a thrice-weekly basis, while some may never call you at all.

Some brides may need lots of emotional support during the engagement—her future mother-in-law is driving her crazy with requests; she's totally freaked about her fiancé's plans for a bachelor party in Amsterdam—and some brides may remain cool as cucumber until they say "I do." So the best advice, aside from fulfilling all your "traditional" duties, is to be flexible. Be patient. And as always, be a good friend.

Bridesmaid Controversy

Of course, there may be circumstances that will prevent you from being the best bridesmaid you can be. You may be tempted to say no to the bride's initial request or to go back and tell her you've reconsidered. Or you may be waiting for a request to be a bridesmaid, which has not been forthcoming. Tread carefully here. Many a friendship has been compromised due to bridesmaid controversy.

Bridesmaid controversy can take on many forms. The following scenarios are some of the most common.

The Surprise Request

The surprise request can come from a huge range of surprising sources—that grammar school pal you haven't seen or talked to in five years, the third cousin you've never gotten along with, or the coworker who considers you her best friend, even though you're content with simply being colleagues. The surprise request will throw you for a loop, and while it's an honor that someone feels so strongly about you, it's also a commitment you're not quite sure you're up to.

Advice: It's never a bad idea to follow the old golden rule, and do unto others as you would have them do unto you. If you can, accept the request with grace and serve out your duties with enthusiasm. However, if you've been asked by someone you simply don't get along with (or no longer have contact with), or if you think you won't be able to fulfill your obligations, it's probably best to respectfully decline now—rather than let down the bride (and the other bridesmaids) later. Also, if you believe you've been asked for the wrong reasons—for example, she's just seeking warm bodies who can afford those Vera Wang dresses—you may be similarly inclined to decline.

FACT

Surprised about that bridesmaid request from a long-lost friend? Consider it an excuse to reignite a waning friendship. What better way to revive a relationship?

The Family Obligation

Your brother's fiancée—you're trying, really trying to like her—has suddenly asked you to be one of her bridesmaids. Just attending the wedding, you thought, would be bad enough—now you have to actually put some *effort* into it. What to do?

Advice: When it comes to family, all bets are off. This person will be related to you for the rest of your life–which means there's no avoiding her, now or later. Suck it up. Some things are simply obligations in life, and this is one of them.

The Poorly Timed Request

You're about to leave on your intricately planned six-month sabbatical to Europe, and your college roommate asks you to be a bridesmaid. Geographically speaking, you won't be around to help plan or attend any of the showers or preparties; in fact, the wedding date may actually be set for before your scheduled arrival home. Whether it's this scenario or a similar one, circumstances such as travel, pregnancy, or work commitments may prevent you from fully committing to the role of bridesmaid.

ALERT!

Beware the bride who relishes creating a bridal "in-crowd" that excludes everyone else. For some brides, forming a bridal party is akin to forming a clique in the sixth grade—a chance to publicly avenge any perceived girlish wrongs and to create new social boundaries forever captured in wedding photos.

Advice: Before agreeing or declining, talk openly with the bride. Tell her your circumstances, and be honest about your level of commitment. If you know you won't be able to contribute your time, planning skills, or finances for whatever reason, let her know in advance rather than setting yourself up for unreasonable expectations, just because you have a hard time saying no. Of course, most women these days have busy lives and full schedules—don't bow out just because you think it will interfere with, say, your time-share in the Hamptons. Be reasonable.

You're Totally Broke

Maybe you're just out of college and can barely scrape by. You could be recently unemployed, have just lost a bundle in the stock market, or be inundated with medical bills. Whatever the reason, you simply can't afford any extras right now—which includes expenses like a bridesmaid dress, a shower, or a bachelorette party.

Advice: Once again, before declining or accepting, talk honestly with the bride. Explain your situation—she's bound to understand. Perhaps she'll offer to purchase your bridesmaid attire, or she'll tell you her aunts are throwing her a shower, anyway. Most likely she'll be more concerned about your participating in her special day than with the money you're able to shell out. Of course, don't decline just because you would rather spend $500 on that new Calvin Klein suit you've had your eye on. There's no doubt the bride and everyone else will see through your ruse pretty clearly.

You Haven't Been Asked

You assumed you would be asked. After all, you've been best friends with the bride since the third grade, and you've always said you'd be bridesmaids in the other's wedding. Yet that phone call has yet to come, and you know for a fact she's already asked two of your other friends. You're worried that maybe you're not going to be included, after all.

Advice: Give it some time. Even if she's already asked others, she may be waiting until the time is right to ask you–perhaps she wants to ask you in person. Or, if she hasn't asked anyone yet, she may have decided not to have a large bridal party–maybe she's still deciding on the style of her wedding.

ESSENTIAL

Being a bridesmaid is not necessarily a reciprocal duty. Just because you've been a bridesmaid for someone doesn't mean you're obligated to ask her to be in your bridal party—and vice versa.

Of course, there's always that possibility that she won't ask you at all–a situation that can be dealt with in a couple of ways. If you know, for instance, that you have grown apart over the years, deep down you may recognize that your nonparticipation may be justified, so just accept her decision gracefully. On the other hand, if you're completely dumbfounded by why you've been omitted from the proceedings, it may be worth talking to her (in a nonaccusatory manner, of course). Otherwise you risk misunderstandings, and possible long-term resentment, over a situation that's often better resolved with a simple, one-time conversation. Hard as it may be, isn't it worth it to try to iron out any wrinkles in your friendship?

The BQ Test: Bridesmaid Quotient

Now that you've done a little legwork to predict the days ahead, the question is, will you or won't you?

Obviously, the decision to be a bridesmaid is ultimately your own. No one can coerce you into taking on the role. However, remember that it is an honor that you've been asked, and that the woman who's asked you obviously thinks quite highly of you. To decline is a serious step. As a woman, you've probably already realized that this type of perceived slight won't soon be forgotten.

Then again, you may have some very real, practical obstacles preventing you from being the best bridesmaid you can be. Mull over the following considerations to gauge whether you are prepared; then read ahead to determine what's an acceptable excuse–and what is not.

Do You Have What It Takes to Be a Good Bridesmaid?

1. You're about to go out with your girlfriends when your newest squeeze calls for last-minute plans. You're most likely to:

    a. Tell him "yes" and blow off your friends completely.
    b. Ask the guy to join you and your girlfriends.
    c. Tell him no (he called too late anyway), and ask him if you can do it another time.

2. When friends leave you voicemail messages, what's your typical response time?

    a. They're lucky if it's a week.
    b. Usually within forty-eight hours.
    c. Almost always the same day.

3. Which best describes your feelings about weddings?

    a. You don't understand all the fuss, and you fully support eloping.
    b. They're great, but they shouldn't eclipse someone's whole life.
    c. The bigger and fancier, the better.

4. Which best describes your job?

    a. You work like a dog, sixty hours a week or more.
    b. Strictly nine to five.
    c. You don't work–you're supported by your parents and/or husband.

5. When the phone rings, you:

a. Screen calls, only picking up if you're in the mood.
b. Screen calls strictly to avoid certain people (coworkers, annoying family members).
c. Answer every ring.

If your answers were mostly "A," you might need to work on your cooperation skills. You tend to do what suits you when you feel like it, others be damned (or your schedule is just so crazy you have no choice). This may put you into some hot water when it comes to being a bridesmaid, so try to put your own concerns aside—even if they conflict—if others are counting on you to be somewhere or complete a specific task. If you've given your word to do something, be sure that you do it.

If your answers were mostly "B," you're open-minded and know how to compromise—which means you'll probably make a great bridesmaid. You tend to see both sides of an issue, and you don't let your own concerns overshadow commitments you've made to others.

If your answers were mostly "C," you're poised to become Super Bridesmaid. You tend to put others' concerns before your own, a very beneficial trait when it comes to being a great bridesmaid. You're also very enthusiastic about weddings, and you have the time to devote to helping out. Just be careful that others don't take advantage of your giving nature.

Excuses, Excuses

There are good excuses. And there are lame ones. Knowing how to distinguish one from the other is very important when it comes to making the decision to accept (or deny) a post as bridesmaid. While one excuse may be viewed as shallow and small, another may actually be a perfectly legitimate reason preventing you from serving out your duties. The key is recognizing one from the other.

Although instinct can often be your guide, there are times you may need a more objective opinion. Unfortunately Dr. Phil isn't readily available, and Dr. Laura would probably bite your head off. Anyway, it doesn't take a psychologist to determine what's fair versus what's just plain selfish. Read ahead to figure out if your excuse will cut the mustard.

Pushing the Limits

The following may reflect your internal rationalizations only, or they may be reasons you're thinking of presenting to the bride to turn down her request. Either way, if you're considering declining based on any of the following excuses, heed this warning: They're just not good enough.

This is not to suggest that you make up another, better excuse. Rather, if these are the reasons you do not want to be a bridesmaid, you should try your hardest to get over them. They are thoughts and feelings that have been shared by many a bridesmaid before you, but despite it all, they, too, survived–and became better friends in the process. Even if they seem good enough to you, rest assured they will be viewed as irrational and selfish by the bride and everyone she tells (in other words, all the other bridesmaids, her family, the groom's family, and half the wedding guests). So proceed only if you wish to risk being socially ostracized.

Excuse: You don't like the dress she's chosen.

Why it's unacceptable: A bad dress is part and parcel of the bridesmaid tradition across the land. Even a decent dress may be the wrong cut, color, and style for you. A less-than-flattering bridesmaid dress is your birthright as a woman and as a girlfriend. In short, it's the last excuse for declining a request to be a bridesmaid.

Excuse: You don't like wearing dresses, period.

Why it's unacceptable: There are some things you simply have to do for love and friendship. Even if you are almost surgically attached to your jeans and Tevas, a few hours in pastel satin won't kill you.

Excuse: You'd rather spend the dress money on those cute boots you've had your eye on.

Why it's unacceptable: There are always things you'd rather spend your money on than a bridesmaid dress you'll never wear again. But sometimes our disposable income must tend toward the more obligatory. Rationalize it as a charitable donation.

Excuse: You're tired of always being a bridesmaid, never a bride.

Why it's unacceptable: Your day will come. And when it does, you don't want to be remembered as the graceless girl who could think of nothing but her own perceived misfortune. Even if you're going through a rough patch, it's no excuse to deny others their happiness. A selfless attitude now will reflect back on you in the future.

Excuse: You don't think you'll have a date to bring.

Why it's unacceptable: As a bridesmaid, you won't have much time to devote to a date, anyway. The dates of the wedding party, in fact, are often the most neglected and bored wedding guests at the party. Plus, going solo offers the opportunity to find a date for the *next* wedding you'll attend . . .

Excuse: You're pregnant.

Why it's unacceptable: There have been many pregnant bridesmaids. And unless you have specific health-related concerns, or the wedding date falls very late in your pregnancy, the inconvenience of being a pregnant bridesmaid is never a good enough excuse. Plus, dressmakers are experienced in fitting a pregnant bridesmaid, even if the wedding is still four months away and you expect to gain twenty-five more pounds.

Excuse: You're busy.

Why it's unacceptable: So is everyone else. Unless there is a specific conflict that goes above and beyond normal daily stress and obligations, simple busy-ness will not get you off the hook.

 **ALERT!**

> Never lie or create false excuses for turning down a request to be a bridesmaid. Inevitably, you will be found out. At the very least, this is bad PR—you will suffer the long-term consequences of being known as a bad friend. Not to mention garnering a new place of honor on the bride's blacklist.

Bowing Out Gracefully

Even if every fiber of your being is crying out to don pastel satin and carry that bouquet down the aisle, there may simply be some obstacles preventing you from serving. If any of these scenarios describes your situation, remember: Don't decline before having a heart-to-heart chat with the bride. Perhaps your participation is important enough for her to be flexible about your level of commitment or responsibilities.

Excuse: You have very real financial concerns.

You or your husband has been laid off. You have unexpected medical or other bills. Or you are simply living on a shoestring budget. If your financial concerns are real–and you're not just cheaping out to avoid contributing to a shower–then even a few hundred dollars for a dress and preparties will really set you back. Talk to the bride, and explain your situation. She may already have an inkling of what's going on, or she may have no idea and appreciate your honesty.

If she is a good friend, she obviously won't wish to burden you any further. She will either offer to help you with the expenses or will give you the option to decline with impunity.

Excuse: You're geographically challenged.

If you simply can't be where you need to be at the appropriate time without some serious setbacks or major inconveniences, it will be difficult to serve as bridesmaid. You may be spending a semester abroad or living in a far-off city. Or perhaps travel will be impossible due to medical concerns, pregnancy, or very young children. The bride will understand if you can't reasonably get away—the key word being "reasonably."

Excuse: Other obligations won't permit it.

Perhaps you have a long-planned work trip you simply can't miss. Or the wedding is scheduled for the same day as your medical school graduation. Or maybe you've already agreed to be a bridesmaid in another wedding on the same day.

Obviously, conflicts like these will prevent you from being a bridesmaid. Let the bride know as soon as possible about any suspected conflicts. If you are very close, the bride may even opt to change her wedding date, so that you'll be able to attend.

Chapter 2

The Maid of Honor

The maid of honor, a.k.a. "the Alpha girl." The über-bridesmaid. The foreman of the tulle-clad jury. The captain of the in-crowd. Before choking on too many metaphors, here's the upshot: The maid of honor is the bridesmaid in charge. If this is you, congratulations—you'll finally have a chance to show off those leadership skills you developed as sorority president or resident adviser in college. The bride's depending on you, so here's what you need to know.

The Ultimate Maid

Being asked to be maid of honor is the ultimate compliment. This post implies not just that you're a good friend but also that you're a great organizer. Because beyond those reams of silk, satin, and pretty bows lies real work–maid of honor is ultimately a role in which organization comes in much handier than aesthetics (though a sense of style, of course, never goes to waste).

Being maid of honor will also afford you much more responsibility than that of being bridesmaid. But before you begin stressing over the details, first take a moment to bask in the glory. Being someone's maid of honor is a true distinction, and you should feel proud and truly honored to have been asked.

There is no difference between a "maid of honor" and a "matron of honor" other than marital status—a matron is married. To date, there is no commonly used moniker for those seeking a marriage-neutral status, such as "Ms. of honor," for instance.

Once you've finished patting yourself on the back, read ahead to find out how your duties differ–and will require a bit more effort–than that of the rest of the bridesmaids. If you're a bit controlling by nature, you were born for this job–it's your chance to take charge without being questioned. If you're more comfortable as an enthusiastic follower, however, don't fret. This chapter will walk you through all your duties, with ideas to make the job easier no matter what your style or leadership comfort level.

Before the Wedding

Whether you're maid of honor or a bridesmaid, the bulk of your practical, time-intensive duties will come primarily during the engagement period, while the more ceremonial ones will take place on the wedding day itself. But unlike the bridesmaids, the maid of honor still carries some high-profile duties on the wedding day, which will be covered in detail in the next section. But let's take first things first. What exactly are your responsibilities leading up to the wedding?

Obviously, not every maid-of-honor experience is the same, and duties will differ based on the bride's preferences and requests. There are, however, some universal responsibilities you can expect to take on from the start. These range from leading the bridesmaids, to planning parties, to providing emotional support throughout the engagement. The level of each will depend on the bride, the style of wedding, and any other mitigating circumstances.

Bride's Liaison

The umbrella responsibility under which the remainder of your duties will fall is simply that of liaison between the bride and the bridesmaids. Being liaison entails communicating any pertinent information (such as the dates of upcoming preparties, information on the bridesmaid attire, and the whats and whens of the wedding itself) to the rest of the bridesmaid troupe.

It also entails keeping the bridesmaids organized and on schedule with reminders and updates about things like fittings, dress pick ups, and parties. This does not mean that the bride speaks only through you during the course of her engagement, but it does mean that she can count on you to impart any information to the greater mass of maids. If she's got a large number of bridesmaids, your role as information disseminator will be especially important, as the bride will find it much easier to tell one person–you–than to keep track of informing twelve people, while also balancing the rest of her wedding planning tasks.

If the prospect of supervising and organizing a slew of bridesmaids that you may or may not know seems equally daunting to you, try adopting some of the following organizational strategies:

- Immediately get the properly spelled full names, e-mail addresses, and street addresses of all bridesmaids.
- Set up a specific group e-mail list for bridesmaids on your computer–at home and at work.
- If there are more than ten bridesmaids, set up a telephone chain in the event of an emergency, or if information needs to get around quickly.

- Optional: Soon after the engagement is announced, host a get-together for all the bridesmaids to meet and greet (if they don't already know each other). This will break the ice, a fun prewedding activity for the bride. Plus, if you get to know them in person, it will be easier to plan parties, showers, and so on when the time comes.

ESSENTIAL

Being organized is the best skill you can have as maid of honor. Your first duty should be getting all the bridesmaids' pertinent contact info, including first and last names (if you don't already know them), phone number, e-mail address, and street address.

Once you have your communication system set up, it will be easier to perform organizational tasks like directing the bridesmaids to order their dresses, letting them know when the dresses are ready to be fitted and altered, and advising them to pick them up in time for the wedding. In addition, you can ensure they have the rest of their attire ready, including shoes, jewelry, and the proper underwear (strapless bras, for instance). Obviously, they are adults who share the responsibility of getting what they need, on time—but it can't hurt to send them a few friendly little reminders (and, in fact, this is part of your official maid-of-honor duties).

The Dress

As you've probably already gathered, another of the maid of honor's duties is to help shop for the bridesmaid dress and accessories. You'll face one of two scenarios: a bride who knows exactly what color and style dress she wants her maids to wear, or a bride who has no clue and seeks your expert input. If your bride falls into the former category, you hope she's chosen a style that's tremendously flattering, or else you're out of luck. If she falls into the latter, you are very fortunate, as you'll have a strong say in what you'll be wearing on the big day. This is a great opportunity to steer the bride toward a style you like—and can afford. Seize it, and make the most of it.

When helping the bride choose bridesmaid dresses, consider the interests of *all* the bridesmaids. That means avoiding too-revealing or too-sexy styles . . . even if they'd happen to look perfect on you.

Remember, this dress will not only be worn by you. Even though you may be a perfectly proportioned size four, chances are there will be some variation in size among the remaining bridesmaids. As tempting as it may be to choose the red spaghetti-strap number with the plunging neckline, bridesmaids who are, say, particularly large-chested or very small-chested may not feel quite as comfortable in it as you. Nor will most bridesmaids above a size two feel comfortable wearing a mermaid-style sheath. The bottom line? Be sensitive to everyone's comfort, not just your own.

Of course, another option is that the maid of honor dresses differently than the rest of the bridesmaids. This may entail wearing a dress of the same color—in a slightly different style—or wearing the same dress with an added accent piece, such as a flowing scarf or a bolero-style jacket. It's been a popular trend in recent years for the maid of honor to stand out in some way from the rest of the bridesmaids, in which case you'll really be free to choose a dress that's flattering to you. In Chapter 3 we cover specific trends, styles, and colors for bridesmaid dresses in more detail; that information may serve as a starting point to help you wade through all the options, if the bride has given you the green light.

FACT

The maid of honor and the rest of the bridesmaids are responsible for footing the full cost of their bridesmaid attire and accessories.

Of course, the financial responsibility for the dress, shoes, accessories, and jewelry ultimately lies with you. Occasionally a bride has been known to subsidize or pay for her bridesmaids' dresses, but she is rare indeed; definitely set a few bucks aside and expect to pay the full amount for all your attire—and don't forget about special underwear needs, such as hosiery, special bras, or other "support" wear.

The Bride's Attaché

Lucky you. Besides being the bride's liaison to the rest of the bridesmaids, you will serve a dual role as the bride's personal ambassador to the world. Like a real-life ambassador, your duties will take on many and varied functions, depending on the daily circumstances. One day you may be asked to drop off color swatches at the florist; the next you may be called upon to mediate a conflict with the groom (or at least listen while the bride vents). Because diplomacy may so often be called upon during the engagement period, your role as attaché cannot be underestimated, and it cannot be eclipsed by your other, more concrete duties, like planning the shower and bachelorette party.

Basically, the sketchy role of bride's "attaché" will require you to be a good friend. Even if the bride calls upon you to help with details that don't concern you or the bridesmaids directly (for example, the bride asks for help choosing the band or invitations), you should be ready and willing to lend a hand. The best maids of honor have been known to help scout out caterers and other vendors; help the bride shop for her wedding dress; assist in making wedding favors; help address invitations; and otherwise function as the bride's Gal Friday.

Obviously, there is potential for matters to get out of control—daily requests to run errands might prove a bit too demanding after a while. (You do have your own life to live, a fact that is occasionally forgotten by brides in the face of wedding planning.) But in general, be prepared to lend a hand when requested. If you're single, it's good practice for your own wedding; if you're married, it's a chance to lend the bride your hard-won expertise–and to relive the glory days of planning your own wedding.

Party Guest Extraordinaire

Another of the maid of honor's duties is to attend all prewedding parties. These include engagement parties, showers, the bachelorette party (or parties), the bridesmaids' luncheon, and the rehearsal dinner. Obviously, if you live far away it will prove a challenge to attend every single prewedding gathering. And unless you're dealing with a really high-maintenance bride, she will hardly expect you to drop everything and fly in repeatedly prior to the wedding.

ESSENTIAL

As the maid of honor, you can exert some of your influence in planning her shower to be the same weekend as another event—this will help other out-of-town bridesmaids or guests to attend as many events as possible, as well.

What you can do is pick and choose the events you'll be able to attend. For example, if there are two engagement parties, try to get to at least one, and talk to the bride about which one she'd prefer you attend. Also, talk to the bride about potentially consolidating events into one weekend or single time frame—have the shower the same weekend as the bachelorette party, for example, or have multiple events in the week leading up to the wedding.

So what is your role at these parties, anyway? As maid of honor, you will be the bride's right-hand gal. At the engagement party, you want to meet all the people you'll be dealing with over the next few months, including the groomsmen and the groom's close family, and friends (presuming you already know the bride's family). You should also take this early opportunity to get to know any bridesmaids you haven't already met. If you're a college friend of the bride's, for instance, it's possible you've never met her high school friends.

At the showers, you will be in charge of tracking all the bride's gifts by keeping copious notes on who gave what. (You may also delegate this task to one of the other bridesmaids, if you're busy helping in some other capacity, like hosting.) This record-keeping will help the bride after the shower, when she writes thank-you notes for all the gifts she's received. Be sure that you or the bridesmaid handling this task writes down a description of each gift in detail, along with its corresponding gift-giver. In all the excitement, the bride will be hard-pressed to remember these details later, especially if it's a large shower, or if she's had more than one.

You will also probably host (or cohost) one of the bride's showers; the next section describes how to get started. At the bridesmaids' luncheon, you are simply there to enjoy yourself. This event is hosted by the bride in appreciation of the bridal party's help over the course of the engagement.

 **FACT**

At all the wedding preparties, including engagement parties, showers, the bachelorette party, and the rehearsal dinner, the maid of honor should make herself available and accessible to help the bride and her mother wherever needed.

And at the rehearsal dinner, you can make yourself especially useful by helping to organize everyone for the wedding day. You might make sure the key players have transportation for the wedding day; reconfirm wedding-day beauty appointments for the bridesmaids; and ensure all the men know what time they're supposed to show up at the chapel. At all the parties—and at the wedding itself—you should make yourself available to the bride and/or her mother if they should need any last-minute help or troubleshooting.

Party Planning 101

If you don't have much experience hosting parties, as maid of honor you'll get it—fast. That's because two of your official duties are to plan a shower and to plan a bachelorette party for the bride. And while you can certainly solicit the help of other bridesmaids, the bride's mother, or other close friends or relatives, ultimately these events will reflect upon you.

FACT

The Internet can be a great source of help for party planning, with topics ranging from invitations to recipes to decorating tips. There are many sites devoted strictly to entertaining, such as *www.perfectentertaining.com*. You can also check women's interest sites, such as *www.ivillage.com*, for comprehensive coverage on entertaining.

Luckily, there's help. If you haven't the first clue about what you're supposed to do, this chapter—along with Chapters 5 and 7—will help you narrow down your many options, as well as inform you, step by step, of what you need to do. And remember, it never hurts to ask for advice, and there are plenty of women who've gone before you who'd be willing to share it. Tap into the girl network for specific recommendations on caterers, punch recipes, games, or activities—you never know what gems you'll come up with.

Shower Her with Attention

One of the most substantial duties you will have as maid of honor is to plan and coordinate a shower for the bride. This may be a task you choose to take on yourself, or you may decide to enlist the aid of the bridesmaids (financial and organizational).

It's entirely up to you, and you should make your intentions clear–the bridesmaids will look to you to get the ball rolling with the shower plans. Bridal showers generally involve a pattern of serving refreshments, followed by gift-giving, interspersed with party games. The level to which you take each of these is entirely dependent on your preferences (and the bride's), and will vary depending upon your budget and entertaining style. For example, you may wish to host a shower in a restaurant, or you may want to keep things simpler and have it at home, serving just cake and punch.

ALERT!

When planning a shower, choose an option that suits your lifestyle. While a shower in a restaurant may seem easy and elegant, it's also going to be a lot more expensive than hosting a party at home. However, if you just don't have the time or resources to throw a party at home, a restaurant or hall may be just the ticket.

Showers are most commonly held on a Saturday or Sunday, usually in the late morning or early afternoon, but a growing trend is to host a shower on a weeknight or weekend evening. Evening showers are often a bit looser and more casual than the typical ladies' Sunday-afternoon brunch.

Of course, feel free to be as creative as you like—your shower guests certainly won't mind attending a party that's a bit off the beaten path. In recent years, more hosts have been throwing showers with creative themes, such as a wine-tasting tie-in or a Mexican-themed party. Themes might also revolve around specific gifts for the bride, such as a kitchen shower, an outdoors-themed shower, or a "round-the clock" shower. (At a round-the-clock shower, each guest is assigned a specific time of day in the invitation, and is asked to bring a gift that suits that time—7 A.M. would merit a griddle or a coffee maker, for instance, while 10 P.M. would inspire lingerie . . . or a popcorn maker.) See Chapter 5 for specific ideas on creative theme showers, games, and decorations.

ALERT!

Another of the maid of honor's duties entails spreading the word about where the bride is registered. Although some people put cards into the shower invitations indicating bridal registry, certain etiquette sticklers consider this to be in poor taste. To be on the safe side, help spread the information via word-of-mouth.

If you need help planning this event—or financing it—talk to the bridesmaids well in advance of the proposed shower date. Obviously, it would be rude to plan a restaurant shower and then ask the bridesmaids to ante up. You should definitely get their input before planning and demanding anything of them. If you pool your resources, it shouldn't be too expensive to host a tasteful, fun shower than everyone will enjoy—and that the bride will truly appreciate.

Can't figure out how to start planning? The following questions will help you begin narrowing your focus regarding what type of shower you'd like to host:

- What's your budget? Will you need help from the other bridesmaids, or do you want to foot the bill—and throw the party—yourself?
- Is the bride very traditional, or would she appreciate a creative twist?
- Will it be formal or casual?
- Do you feel it's important to serve a full meal?
- Can you cook, or will you get the help of a friend, family member, or caterer?
- Do you have enough space to host it at your own home, or is there another bridesmaid who does? (You can also ask a family member or friend if you can "borrow" their home for the day.)
- Would you prefer for professionals to handle everything, from beginning to end?
- Will you host a "theme" shower?

- Are there unusual circumstances (the bride is pregnant, it's her second wedding)?
- Would you rather host a coed "Jack and Jill" shower? (These have grown increasingly popular, as well, in recent years.)
- Would an evening gathering be better than a daytime one?
- Are there lots of out-of-town guests to invite and accommodate? (Weekends might be best in this case.)
- Do you want to include party games?
- Do you want to incorporate any new traditions?

By answering these questions, you'll begin to narrow down some of the many options. Be sure to consult Chapter 5 for a step-by-step, how-to-plan-a-shower guide, with specific ideas for food, games, and themes.

The Bachelorette Party

So you've planned and hosted a shower with great style and success. Just when you thought you were off the hook, there's one more event to consider—the bachelorette party. This party should be a little easier to plan, as it involves activities you probably do more regularly—a night on the town, for example, or a day at a spa.

The Girls' Answer to Bachelor Parties

The bachelorette party basically developed as a response to the boys' long-revered bachelor party, and it is a relatively recent phenomenon among "the girls"—

after all, why should boys have all the fun? Of course, the bachelorette party that you plan doesn't need to be as raucous as the typical bachelor party . . . but then again, it can be if that's what the bride wants. Which means there's only one way to decide what tone this event should take, and that's to check with the bride.

To an even greater degree than the shower, follow the bride's lead when it comes to planning the bachelorette party. That means you should get a pretty clear indication of her likes and dislikes when it comes to a night of revelry with the girls. Based on her personality and her normal activities, you probably already have some idea of whether she'd like a wild night of bar-hopping or a more subdued spa weekend. If she's not into the bar scene, plunging her into a night of club-hopping and male strippers may make her uncomfortable. But check with her to be sure. The most mild-mannered gal may wish to seize this opportunity to let it all hang out while she's still a swinging single.

Planning Her "Last Hoorah"

Which brings us to planning. As with the shower, you should enlist the help of the bridesmaids, who will probably be eager to add their two cents to coming events. Once you've decided the tone this event will take, you'll be able to narrow down your options.

If you want a more subdued event, for example, you may wish to plan a day on the golf course, an elegant dinner out, or a day of beauty treatments. If you want to plan something a bit wilder, then you may begin considering hiring a limo, ordering a stripper, or even planning a girls' getaway to Las Vegas. Solicit the opinions of the bridesmaids. They may have some inspiration from other bachelorette parties they've attended.

Another factor you may want to consider when planning the bachelorette party is the guest list. If it's going to be, say, you, the bride, and all your college friends, planning the party will pretty much be a no-brainer. But if there are other people involved, who you may not know quite so intimately (or who may have other ideas of what constitutes "fun"), then party planning may prove to be a bit more challenging.

ALERT!

When planning the bachelorette party, definitely follow the bride's wishes. Don't force an evening of wild drinking and partying if she doesn't want it.

For example, one bride in San Diego—we'll call her Sandra—didn't feel right excluding her mother and aunts from her bachelorette party. Sandra is extremely close to these family members, who are a lot of fun, but they're not quite up to the club scene. So the maid of honor and bridesmaids decided to plan something that everyone could enjoy—a night of cards and cocktails at one of the bridesmaids' homes. Knowing the "older generation" would get a kick out of it, they did order a male stripper. But this is not recommended for every mixed-generation bachelorette party (or every bride, for that matter).

The lesson here is to keep every guest in mind when planning the big soiree. If much of the crowd doesn't drink, then don't revolve activities solely around drinking games or bar-hopping. Or, if only a fraction of the group plays golf, then don't plan a day on the links (even if you and the bride happen to love it). Plan something that everyone can enjoy, or else risk a party that poops out right from the start.

Paying for It

Now that you've got the perfect idea, who pays for this shindig, anyway? Once again, it is you and the rest of the bridesmaid troupe who are responsible for footing the bill. As with the shower, plan a party that fits everyone's budgets. Don't empty your savings account to pay for a party that you really can't afford.

You may also ask the party-goers to contribute. For example, if you're planning a ski weekend, and you're renting a chalet or condo, ask everyone who comes (bridesmaids and other girlfriends) to chip in for the rental cost and to cover their own individual expenses like lift tickets and so on. If you want to spring for *something,* bring food and/or drinks that the group can enjoy over the course of the weekend, and split the cost of the bride's lift tickets and other expenses among the bridesmaids.

There are many elements you can add to a bachelorette party to make it more fun and memorable, including games, decorations, and props. When planning the party, you may wish to delegate one responsibility to each bridesmaid. For instance, one bridesmaid can be in charge of buying props, one in charge of buying cocktails or mixers, and one in charge of organizing games or activities.

FACT

You are not expected to foot the bill for the bachelorette party by yourself. Instead, ask if everyone will pitch in a little for key costs like the limo rental, hotel rooms, or a stripper.

Make sure everyone saves her receipts—then total all the expenses and split the bill evenly after the party. As maid of honor, you may wish to take charge of the financial elements if all the bridesmaids are participating.

Not Just for Girls

Another bachelorette party option may include merging the girls with the boys—creating one all-encompassing bachelor and bachelorette party. Obviously not every bride and groom will go for this idea, but in recent years it's become more and more common for the party to be coed, or for the two "parties" to meet up and become one at a certain point in the evening. Maybe your group of friends isn't big on separating by gender, or the bride has a lot of male friends she wouldn't want to exclude from her celebration. Whatever the reason, the bachelorette/bachelor party is another opportunity to celebrate a fun evening (or day) with everyone involved in the wedding.

The Wedding Day

So you've completed all your prewedding day duties with great style and success. After all this planning and prepartying, you can hardly believe the main event hasn't happened yet. But here it is, and your responsibilities continue. After all, this is what you've all been working up to.

The wedding day can be very tense and stressful for the bride—and you, lucky girl, can make it much easier for her. From the moment you wake up, your job will be to attend to the bride's needs and concerns. Some brides may not want anything from you except to enjoy your company, while others may have you running around like a feline on catnip. The more organized the bride's been, the less you'll probably have to do—pending any unexpected circumstances like weather, no-show vendors, or other wedding-related disasters.

The Morning of the Wedding

If the wedding is in the afternoon, most likely you, the bride, and the bridesmaids are planning to use the hours leading up to the ceremony to get ready. This may involve appointments at the salon, massages, and manicures and/or pedicures–a veritable beauty bonanza.

As maid of honor, you should have everyone's schedules written down to refer to, especially if you, the bride, or the bridesmaids have multiple appointments. This way you can serve as the go-to girl for the bridesmaids and for the salon and spa that you're visiting. To be sure everyone knows where to be and when, you may consider giving each bridesmaid her own written wedding-day itinerary at the rehearsal dinner. This is a particularly helpful strategy if there are lots of activities and appointments you'll need to keep track of on the day of the wedding.

ESSENTIAL

It's a good idea to include transportation on your itinerary—how each girl is getting to each place. This will keep Bridesmaid No. 2 from driving off and leaving you—or the bride!—stranded at the hair salon.

Once you're all ready and beautiful, your next job is to organize the bridesmaids' bouquets when they arrive from the florist. Sort them out and confirm that each bridesmaid has her own bouquet, and that none have been forgotten. If there is any problem with the flowers, troubleshoot with the florist on the bride's behalf.

Many brides choose to have as many photographs as possible taken before the wedding ceremony. You may wish to suggest she set aside forty-five minutes to an hour before the wedding to take pictures with her parents and the bridesmaids, cutting some of the post-wedding photo time you'll need. Plus you'll all be looking your freshest and best before the day's many activities begin.

If you need to, help organize the progression of photos throughout the wedding day. For example, the bride may wish to have formal portraits taken with her parents, you, all the bridesmaids, and her flower girls, separately as well as together. Advise her to give a written list to the photographer to ensure none of these are forgotten.

The Ceremony

The maid of honor's most important ceremonial duties involve keeping the bride looking good and feeling organized. These duties begin the moment you arrive at the ceremony site. As soon as you get there, take a moment to rearrange the bride's dress, train, veil, hair, and makeup, if necessary. Oftentimes the car ride can result in a bunched-up train, or wind can mess that perfectly-coiffed 'do.

During the ceremony itself, your responsibilities include the following:

- Walking down the aisle, immediately preceding the bride.

- Artfully arranging the bride's dress, train, and veil when she reaches the end of the aisle. You'll want to help her ensure that her dress looks perfectly arranged for photographs. If it's an especially long train, you may wish to have another bridesmaid help you lay it out behind her.
- Holding on to the groom's ring, and giving it to the bride at the appropriate time during the ceremony. Be sure to keep it in a very safe place–such as your thumb–so you won't lose it or forget to carry it down the aisle.
- Holding the bride's bouquet during the ceremony. This means placing your bouquet on a chair or church pew, and holding hers so the flowers don't get crushed or bent.
- Acting as a formal witness to the marriage. This involves signing the marriage license and any religious documents that may be included in the formal wedding ceremony.

ESSENTIAL

Obviously, you will be the subject of many photographs during the ceremony, as well. As if there's not enough to think about, don't forget to make an effort to stand up straight and keep a neutral expression or smile on your face, or be ready to get caught on film in some unflattering positions.

After the Wedding Ceremony

Congratulations–you've done your duty. The bride is successfully married and looking her best. But just when you thought your wedding-day tasks were done, there's more.

Your first responsibility immediately follows the wedding ceremony, and it includes participating in the receiving line. This is when the bride, groom, their parents, and sometimes the honor attendants (maid of honor and best man) stand and greet all the guests who've come to the wedding ceremony. The bride may ask that you participate in the receiving line, or she may prefer you mingle among the guests–it's up to her whether you'll be part of the line itself.

If you are, you need simply stand there and smile. No one really knows what to say in the ten to twenty seconds allotted to each receiving line exchange (and chances are that many of these exchanges will involve virtual strangers), so think of a few throwaway lines beforehand like "Great to see you," "Beautiful dress," or "Gorgeous day" to keep the guests occupied with small talk, should they falter.

Let the Good Times Roll

Finally, the reception. You can let loose, find your date, and forget about responsibility for the rest of the night, now, right? Wrong! This gig ain't over until the bride manages to get out of her dress (that's right, you may even have to help her there). But before you can even think about that inevitability, you've got a few more responsibilities to honor.

Winding Down Your Duties

If the reception is at a different location than the ceremony, you'll want to help the bride freshen up as soon as you arrive. That means assisting her with any touchups to makeup, hair, dress or veil, and bustling her dress if necessary (bustling is usually quite simple—there are loops that correspond to buttons on the dress). By now, the bride will also probably have to use the bathroom—and will definitely require your help with this immodest task, or risk dropping her pristine white gown in the toilet. Be prepared to also help rearrange stockings and underwear once she's done—it's tough to be flexible when you're wearing a ten-pound dress.

Aside from these more intimate duties, there is also a public role you, as the maid of honor, will need to fulfill at the reception, including general hosting, dancing with the best man (if there is a wedding-party dance), and collecting any wedding-gift envelopes from guests. The bride will probably have a designated envelope-collector—her father, the best man, or maybe you—to consolidate these envelopes as they are offered. If you are the one assigned this task, be extremely careful about keeping track of them—most will contain checks or even cash gifts.

Reception Toast

For many years, tradition has held that the best man give a speech before the meal. But as with the bachelor party, why should the boys have all the fun? In recent years, it's become increasingly common to hear a toast from the maid of honor as well as the best man. And why not? You've got as much to say—and probably much more, in fact—as the best man.

ALERT!

If you dread speaking in public, you've got no obligation to give a toast to the happy couple. It's your prerogative to keep your lip zipped.

If you do plan to say a few words, let the bride, groom, and best man know in advance, so they can pass the mike to you at the appropriate time. This could be either before or after the best man's toast.

But what should you say? Well, that's entirely up to you. Tell a funny anecdote about the bride and groom, or tell a sentimental story about the bride and her family. The following tips will help you write and deliver a speech the wedding guests won't soon forget:

- Brainstorm ideas to develop your theme. Consider how the bride and groom met, the first time you met the groom, your history with the bride and her family, or events that emerged during the engagement. Your toast/speech can be funny or touching—say what feels most natural and appropriate for this wedding.

- Consider whether you'd like to precede or follow the best man's speech with your own. Do you want the audience warmed up beforehand, or would you rather dazzle them right off the bat?
- Consider your audience. This is a diverse group that probably ranges in age from eight to eighty. Try to appeal to every guest with universal themes, references, and speech patterns. Avoid slang terms and repeated use of phrases including "like," "you know," and "um."
- Start with a catchy opening. It can be a joke or a quick anecdote, but it should capture the attention of the guests right away.
- Maintain eye contact. Don't stare at your cue cards or at the table. Try to keep your gaze focused on various guests around the room. (But consult cards if you need to.)
- Remember to stand up straight and avoid fidgeting.
- Project your voice, especially if there isn't a microphone.
- Take a few deep breaths before you begin your speech to relieve the butterflies.
- Practice, practice, practice! Rehearse your speech in front of a mirror, or consult a trusted friend for an honest opinion. There's no better way to get it just right at the wedding.
- Never include off-color jokes, racy stories, or confidential information in your speech. Keep the subject matter positive and upbeat.

- Keep your toast brief, just a few minutes long. Too long-winded, and you'll lose the attention of your audience, especially if yours is just one of many toasts/speeches.

Sharing Your Duties

So you're sharing the maid of honor duties with another person. There are a number of good reasons this may be so. Perhaps the bride has two sisters or friends and can't choose between them, or perhaps she's decided to include both a maid of honor and a matron of honor.

No matter what the reason, these circumstances should only make your job easier–two heads are always better than one. To keep things running smoothly, be sure to open the lines of communication with the other honor attendant right away, so that you avoid duplicating tasks and/or stepping on each other's toes.

If you're sisters or friends, you'll no doubt be in close contact already. But if you're not especially close–she's a friend of the bride's from childhood, for example, and you're a friend from college–organizing will present more of a challenge. Be sure to keep each other updated on the progress of any plans, such as for the shower or bachelorette party–if possible, plan them together. Or split up the events, and take responsibility for one party apiece.

But above all, remember to have fun–it's an honor to share in this exciting celebration with the bride!

Chapter 3

Show Her the Money

The first question on many new bridesmaids' minds is usually—and understandably—one of finances. And while most brides do try to be cost-conscious, you may unfortunately encounter the exception to that rule—the bride to whom money is no object when it comes to her dream day . . . and who assumes everyone else feels the same way. This chapter covers a variety of contingencies, including some cost estimates for each. It also offers up some money-saving tips for bridesmaids who care to save a buck or two.

What's the Bottom Line?

As you serve as bridesmaids for multiple weddings, you'll find they have one thing in common—they're all different. Every wedding and bridesmaid experience varies based on all the details of that particular wedding, including the wedding's location, the level of formality, the style of dress, and any other special requests that the bride makes. This chapter breaks down these differences, providing a breakdown of average expenses for some of the more common nuptial scenarios. It also provides estimates for more controllable expenses, such as the shower and the bachelorette party costs.

ALERT!

Understanding the financial responsibilities of the wedding from the outset will help you budget properly. Where possible, avoid using credit cards, as you'll pay a whopping interest rate that will overinflate your expenses. (For instance, that $200 bridesmaid dress will end up costing you $300 once the interest has compounded.)

The Out-of-Town Affair

You're a bridesmaid of the world. You left town for college, traveled abroad, and moved to an exciting new city—or two—after you graduated. You've got close friends in every port, from every stage of your life—

grammar school, high school, summer camp, college, graduate school, your working years. Not to mention family members who've also moved around to different areas of the country—or the world.

That means you'll inevitably be attending weddings in every port, as well. Lucky you. What's more fun than discovering a new place—or rediscovering an old one? Of course, with the good sometimes comes the challenging, because travel inevitably means additional expenses. But hey—it's for a good cause, and a good friend.

If you're a bridesmaid, that may even mean multiple trips to the city/town of choice—one for the wedding, and one or two additional trips for the showers, bachelorette party, or engagement party. If it's a faraway destination, obviously, the expenses can add up quickly. The following is an estimated breakdown of bridesmaid expenses for the typical out-of-town wedding.

Costs for an out-of-town wedding	
Dress:	$200
Alterations:	$50
Shoes:	$50
Accessories/jewelry:	$50
Hair and makeup:	$100–$150
Shower:	$100
Bachelorette party:	$100
Shower gift:	$40
Wedding gift:	$100–$200
Shower travel costs:	$300–$700

Costs for an out-of-town wedding (continued)	
Wedding travel costs:	\$300–\$700 (double that if you're bringing a date/husband)
Hotel costs (wedding):	\$100–\$200 per night
Additional travel costs (tipping, room service, and so on):	\$50
Total:	**\$1,540–\$2,590 (\$3,290+ including date/spouse)**

In-Town Hoopla

So, you're lucky enough to be serving a bride close to home. Being in close proximity makes everything easier, from organizing parties to paying for expenses. Plus, responsibilities like dress fittings won't take on Herculean logistical proportions, as you attempt to time the dress's arrival with the shower (so you can pick it up while you're in the bride's hometown), along with scheduling enough time before the wedding for alterations. (Of course, many shops will deliver your dress, too—for a cost. Expect to pay around \$25–\$50 if the dresses are purchased at a shop but shipped to your home.)

Fortunately, these are out-of-towner concerns, and your bride's wedding is *in* town for this scenario. That means many of your bridesmaid tasks can be performed at your leisure—plus, you'll save money on travel expenses. Here's a breakdown of the expenses you can expect for the wedding that's close to home:

Costs for an in-town wedding	
Dress:	$200
Alterations:	$50
Shoes:	$50
Accessories/jewelry:	$50
Hair and makeup:	$100–$150
Shower:	$100
Bachelorette party:	$100
Shower gift:	$40
Wedding gift:	$100–$200
Shower travel costs:	$0
Wedding travel costs:	$0
Hotel costs (wedding):	$0 per night
Additional travel costs (tipping, room service, etc.):	$0
Total:	**$790–$940 (a significant savings from the out-of-town wedding)**

The Theme Wedding

Perhaps the bride has decided to plan a theme wedding—a medieval wedding, for example, or a Victorian wedding. Obviously, finding the appropriate outfit and achieving the "look" is what will make this wedding stand out from traditional, non-theme weddings. This unique look is the factor that can translate into unique costs, as well.

The problem with estimating these costs, however, is that they are extremely difficult to predict—especially with variations in the extravagance and availability of costumes for certain themes. However, the following provides a rough estimate for the bridesmaid participating in a theme wedding:

Costs for a theme wedding	
Dress/Attire:	$100–$400 (a rental costume may fall on the lower end of the cost spectrum, while purchasing that great vintage dress will raise it)
Alterations:	$50
Shoes:	$50
Accessories/jewelry:	$100
Hair and makeup:	$100–$150
Shower:	$100–$150
Bachelorette party:	$100–$150
Shower gift:	$40
Wedding gift:	$100–$200
Shower travel costs:	$300–$700
Wedding travel costs:	$300–$700 (double that if you're bringing a date/husband)
Hotel costs (wedding):	$100–$200 per night
Additional travel costs (tipping, room service, etc.):	$50
Total:	**$1,390–$2,540 (no date) to $3,240 (with date)**

(Included are travel costs, in the event this wedding is also out of town.)

As you can see, the most significant variation you'll find when dealing with a theme wedding is in the cost of your bridesmaid's attire. This may be a good thing or a bad thing. If the bride is planning a Renaissance wedding, for example, you may end up spending less than you would on a traditional bridesmaid's dress if, for example, you'll be renting an outfit from a costume shop (expect to pay $50 to $100).

FACT

A "theme" wedding incorporates an unusual, creative element into the wedding tradition. Popular themes include medieval weddings and Cinderella weddings, whereas more unusual themes may include underwater weddings or hot-air balloon celebrations.

On the other hand, if the bride is throwing a fairy-tale princess wedding, you may be saddled with additional costs for more extravagant bridesmaid dresses, tiaras, special shoes, and other jewelry you might not otherwise have required. Or, if she's throwing a funky disco wedding, you may feel compelled to buy that vintage Halston dress that you just *know* saw the likes of Studio 54 and needs to be put back into the circuit. So, as you've probably ascertained, a theme wedding is a bit more difficult to predict, as the attire can range dramatically from one theme wedding to the next.

Note we've also accounted for a slight increase in the shower and bachelorette party costs. This has been included in case you're inspired to throw a shower or bachelorette party that coordinates with the wedding theme. Incorporating a theme into either of these parties will probably cost a bit more, with potential for additional expenses like a special location (the grounds of a medieval fair, for instance), or for decorations that will reflect the theme (disco ball, multitiered dance floor). Obviously, though, this will ultimately be up to you and the rest of the bridesmaids to decide on and budget for.

FACT

Expenses like the shower and bachelorette party are more controllable than expenses such as the bridesmaid's attire. Work with the other bridesmaids to plan a party that suits all your budgets.

The Destination Wedding

There's a difference between destination weddings and out-of-town weddings—destination weddings will probably end up costing you a lot more. But on the flip side, you'll probably also get a lot more out of it, as destination weddings are often like mini-vacations that you'll enjoy beyond the wedding celebration.

A destination wedding is a wedding that's generally defined by "getting away from it all." They're usually smaller than the traditional gathering, and they may include immediate family, close friends, and the wedding party. Often they're held somewhere exotic, such as a tropical location, ski resort, foreign city, or some faraway enclave.

Destination weddings have grown in popularity in recent years, and couples who hold them typically want a wedding that's a bit more intimate—or way off the beaten track. And while destination weddings are usually smaller and more intimate—including just close family and friends—there are exceptions to every rule. Some destination weddings are simply traditional weddings, transplanted to a more exotic locale.

So what does the destination wedding mean for you? Well, a number of things—you'll be traveling somewhere you may have never been before, and you'll probably be staying longer than you would for a traditional weekend wedding. This translates, obviously, into higher costs.

There is one exception, and that's if the bride and groom (or their families) are paying the travel and accommodation costs themselves. If it's a very small group that's attending, for instance, the wedding couple may use the funds they would have spent on a 300-guest wedding for the travel and hotel costs of the group they've invited. But don't assume or expect this. Obviously, travel and accommodation costs for a group of even ten people can add up quickly.

So what can you expect? Let's assume the wedding will be held at an all-inclusive resort in the Caribbean—a very popular location for destination weddings. The wedding couple, their family, and their friends are invited to spend the five days leading up to the wedding at the resort; the fifth day will culminate with the wedding. How much will this cost? Here's an estimate.

Costs for a destination wedding	
Dress:	$200
Alterations:	$50
Shoes:	$0 (it's a barefoot-on-the-beach wedding)
Accessories/jewelry:	$50
Hair and makeup:	$100–$150
Shower:	$100
Bachelorette party:	$100
Shower gift:	$40
Wedding gift:	$100–$200
Shower travel costs:	$0 (we'll assume it was in your hometown)
Wedding travel costs and accommodations:	$1,500–$2,500 (double that if you're bringing a date/husband)
Additional travel costs (tipping, room service, etc.):	$50
Total:	**$2,290–$3,440 (no date); up to $6,010 (with date)**

The Designer Wedding

So you have a friend in your life who is very cool, very stylish, and very, well, loaded. And now she's asked you to be her bridesmaid. Which is great, except that while she's been shopping Prada, you've been shopping Penney's. You can only imagine the designer bridesmaid dresses, shoes, and accessories she's going to choose for her attendants.

ALERT!

Just because the bride has expensive tastes doesn't mean you need to buy an extravagant wedding gift. You should always give only what you can afford, and you can choose something elegant and tasteful in any price range.

You hope she'll realize early that not all of her bridesmaids are Rockefellers, like her. And she will make her choices accordingly. But chances are that she still won't be choosing the cheapest meal on the menu—and unfortunately, you'll still have to swallow it. You may also face some slightly higher shower and bachelorette party costs, particularly if the majority of the other bridesmaids (or the maid of honor) share her lifestyle. So what will that mean? An increase on the average prices of all your attire, from head to toe, plus parties.

Costs for a designer wedding	
Dress:	$350–$500
Alterations:	$50–$100
Shoes:	$100–$400

Costs for a designer wedding (continued)	
Accessories/jewelry:	$200
Hair and makeup:	$150–$200
Shower:	$200
Bachelorette party:	$100–$1,500 ($1,500?! Yes, if the party's in Vegas.)
Shower gift:	$40
Wedding gift:	$100–$200
Shower travel costs:	$0 (we'll assume it's in your hometown)
Wedding travel costs:	$0
Accommodations:	$0
Additional travel costs (tipping, room service, etc.):	$0
Total:	**$1,290–$3,340 (add in an extra $1,000+ if the wedding is out of town)**

The Budget-Conscious Wedding

So your bride's always been thrifty? Then maybe she'll exploit her budget-conscious nature in deference to her bridesmaids, too. Though you shouldn't count on past thriftiness to be an indication of wedding costs—some of the biggest penny-pinchers in "real" life know no boundaries for their own weddings.

Or maybe your bride is just extra considerate of the financial constraints of her closest friends and family members. Regardless, this bride is working hard to keep costs down, and she will at the very least give you options. For example, she'll tell you that a trip to the salon for wedding-day hair and makeup is optional; or the black strappy sandals you already own are perfectly fine to wear. Thus, your expenses can end up being dramatically lower than many of the earlier scenarios.

One exception is travel expenses. If you've got to travel, there's not much the bride can do, short of covering your expenses, which you should not count on. She may, however, seek out free accommodations for you among family or friends.

Costs for the budget-conscious wedding	
Dress:	$75–$150
Alterations:	$25–$50
Shoes:	$0–$40
Accessories/jewelry:	$0
Hair and makeup:	$0–$75
Shower:	$100
Bachelorette party:	$100
Shower gift:	$40
Wedding gift:	$100–$200
Shower travel costs:	$0 (we'll assume it's in your hometown)
Wedding travel costs and accommodations:	$0
Additional travel costs (tipping, room service, etc.):	$0
Total:	**$440–$755 (tack on $1,000+ if the wedding is out of town)**

Obviously, the budget-conscious bride can keep costs much lower than the average by allowing bridesmaids to wear their own shoes (or to buy them cheaply), wear their own accessories, and by not demanding professional hair and makeup services. She'll also make an effort to choose a less expensive dress—maybe even an "off the rack" dress from a department store or specialty store, like Banana Republic or Ann Taylor. All of these strategies will cut costs significantly, as well as allow the bridesmaids to exhibit some of their own personal style as a by-product.

Cost-Cutting Measures

No matter what the style of wedding—destination, theme, or otherwise—there are still some strategies you can use to cut the costs estimated in the previous sections. They are meant to achieve the same—or virtually the same—results but at a lower cost. In other words, we're not suggesting you boycott the bride's choice of dress, or defy the bride's wishes for a special up-do (as unreasonable as that may feel to you). The following strategies are simply meant to help you cut corners in the areas where you'll be likely to get away with it.

The Bridesmaid Attire

The bridesmaid dress is the bridesmaid dress. Once the bride has chosen it, there's little any of the bridesmaids can do about it beside complain, pout, and sulk (never to the bride's face, of course). So unfortunately, there's little you'll be able to do to cut this expense. However, you may be able to cut some of the ancillary attire costs, including the following.

Alterations

Never go to a bridal salon or dress shop for alterations, which, like most wedding vendors, will charge you more than the competitive market rate. Most any independent tailor or seamstress will charge significantly less. If you already know a trusted seamstress, bring the dress to her for any hemming or alterations. If you don't know of anyone offhand, ask for recommendations from the other bridesmaids, family members, or friends.

FACT

Most bridesmaid dresses are cut on the smallish side, so don't worry if you end up ordering them a size (or two or three) larger than your regular size. Carefully follow the salon's guidelines for taking your measurements. It's a lot easier (and cheaper) to tailor a dress down than it is to make it larger.

Shoes

If the bride hasn't specified her choice in shoes, ask if you can wear a pair you already own. If she has her heart set on dyeables, see if she'll agree to purchasing them at a less expensive store like Payless, which often charges half what other shoe stores do. Or, ask if she'd mind if you re-dye a pair that you already own in a color to match the dress. (Obviously, the store won't be able to dye a pair of emerald green shoes pink; use your judgment here.)

Accessories

Often the bride will give attendants necklaces and/or earrings—or an evening bag—as a special gift before the wedding, so the bridesmaids will be uniformly accessorized. If she doesn't offer accessories as a gift, and she doesn't specify a preference in what accessories you wear, then you have lots of options. You can go for a simple look, with little to no jewelry; you might try wearing a classic piece you already own, such as a strand of pearls; you can raid your mother's or sister's jewelry box for a fun piece; or you can buy something new—on sale—at a costume jewelry shop or department store. If you do buy something, the key is picking a piece you'll wear again and again—not just with your bridesmaid dress.

Hair and Makeup

If the bride wishes to schedule group appointments for professionally coiffed hair or makeup application on the morning of the wedding, find out in advance what the salon will charge for each service. If you can't afford it, opt out (if the bride has given you a choice), and meet up with the group afterward. You can do your own hair and makeup, go to a salon that you know will charge less, or have a talented friend or sister do the honors.

Travel Costs

If you're traveling to your wedding destination, flying will most likely be the biggest travel-related expense. The first thing you may want to consider is driving to your destination (if possible). If you're used to flying, it might be an inconvenience, but it could also save you a lot of money. For instance, a flight from Buffalo to Philadelphia for two people costs an average of $600; saving that much could be well worth the seven-hour drive. Plus, if you drive, you'll save on the cost of a rental car once you get there—as good as another $100 to $200 in your pocket.

If you do decide to fly—or have little choice, based on the distance of your destination—consider "alternate" destinations served by lower-cost airlines. For instance, if you're flying to Washington, D.C., you may consider flying into Baltimore/Washington International instead of Dulles or Reagan National Airport, to take advantage of cheaper flights offered by discount airlines like Southwest. It may be a little farther from your final destination, but it could also save you hundreds of dollars.

ESSENTIAL

Try using Web sites like *www.orbitz.com* and *www.expedia.com* to find low fares. Some lower-cost airlines (like Southwest) are not included in these sites, so be sure to also check them for lower fares before booking.

You should also consider strategies that include things like flying on less popular days—thus less expensive—like Saturday and Tuesday, and making your reservations well in advance. Also consider using frequent flyer miles or credit card points to redeem for free or less expensive airline tickets.

If you do fly, you'll need some way to get around once you get there. If you decide to rent a car, see if any of the other bridesmaids would like to share the rental—after all, you'll be running around doing the same things all weekend anyway. Public transportation may be a more practical solution, especially if you're staying in a city like New York, where a rental car can be more of a hindrance than a help. Carry subway maps and the name of a car service in case you get stuck or lost.

Affordable Accommodations

If the wedding is out of town, chances are the bride or groom's family has sent information on recommended accommodations. Often, they've already negotiated a discount rate at a hotel based upon the volume of guests the wedding will guarantee, so this may be your lowest rate for the area. But if it still seems high, feel free to do some detective work on other nearby hotels, bed-and-breakfasts, or motels. You may discover accommodations that suit your budget much better.

If you give yourself enough time, you may wish to try a Web site like *www.priceline.com,* where you can get a significantly lower rate by "quoting your own price." The site works by listing hotels and motels by ballpark price and number of stars; you then bid on that property with an amount that you feel willing to pay. If the hotel doesn't accept it, they'll tell you within an hour, and after a certain amount of time passes you can try again.

ESSENTIAL

Check out the local bed-and-breakfasts for accommodations that are often less expensive—and more charming and personalized—than chain hotels and motels.

You may also wish to double up with a friend or a bridesmaid to cut the cost of your hotel room in half. Hey, you did it for four years in college. Why not relive those days with a roommate? You'll inevitably spend little time in your hotel room anyway, with all the activities and responsibilities the weekend will bring.

Obviously, the least expensive accommodations are with friends or family. Get the word out that you'll be in town, and hope you'll be extended an invitation. If you get one, be sure to bring a hostess gift (flowers, candy, baked goods–any thoughtful, small gift will do)–and be considerate during your stay–or don't be surprised if you're not invited back. And don't forget to send a thank-you note after you get home!

Low-Priced Parties

Who ever said a good party has to be expensive? The success of a party ultimately depends on the guest list and a good vibe—whether you're drinking Coors Light or Cristal shouldn't have much of an influence.

Ultimately, how and where you throw a shower and bachelorette party is not solely your decision. The maid of honor generally spearheads this process, with financial and organizational help from the bridesmaids. That means you should all get together—in person, by phone, or via e-mail—to begin deciding the best course of action. See the next section in this chapter regarding the nuts and bolts of shower planning.

With that said, there are certain money-saving strategies you can adopt while planning the shower. A shower at someone's home will be much less expensive than a restaurant or country-club shower, for instance, and a shower with snacks and refreshments only will be easier on the budget than serving a full meal.

A home-based bachelorette party can be much less expensive than a night on the town, as well—and no less fun. See Chapter 6 for specific ideas on creative bachelorette parties you can have at home, along with ideas for a fun evening out.

Gifts in Good Taste

With all these other expenses, you're still required to give a shower and a wedding gift? Obviously, a gift is never a requirement—it's a voluntary offering. But it is appropriate for bridesmaids to give a gift for both the shower and the wedding, and you're sure to feel awkward if you're the only bridesmaid who opts not to.

If you're strapped for cash after all these other expenses, you do have some options. Do you have a special talent like photography, painting, or sewing? Give a homemade gift like a framed or mounted photo, an original watercolor, or an embroidered pillow. Only the most hardhearted of brides wouldn't love a gift that's so personal and unique.

ESSENTIAL

The amount you spend on a gift is not important. Rather, it's the thought and ability behind the gift you're giving that should be valued. Of course, that's easier said than believed. But remember, they are offerings of goodwill, not obligations.

Fashion File

So you feel informed about what the dress will cost–but what will it look like? Luckily, the days of awful bridesmaid dresses with flounces, bows, and fabric in all the wrong places are virtually over, as many designers have jumped on the opportunity to create pretty, interesting, and largely flattering dresses that reflect current trends and tastes. The bad rap does still remain to some extent, however; likely due to the fact that six women of different shapes and sizes seldom all look fabulous in a single dress style.

One Size Fits All?

And there's the rub. Fortunately, dress designers are starting to realize this fact as well, and current trends are reflecting the inevitable fact that all women will not fit well in the same dress. Thus, bridesmaid fashion's most current trend is the rise of the two-piece dress. These dresses typically feature tops and bottoms that can be bought and ordered separately, in the appropriate size. Which means the bridesmaid who's a size twelve on top and an eight on the bottom won't have to settle for a dress that needs heavy-duty alterations. It usually results in dresses that fit and flatter much better, as well.

Variations on a Theme

Another recent trend is the rise of "variations on a theme." This is when a specific dress color is chosen—usually from one dress designer, so the color remains consistent—and bridesmaids are given license to choose the dress style they feel most comfortable in. This works because designers typically offer a variety of dresses in the same choice of colors.

Here's an example of how it works. First, the bride chooses a color and designer—say, midnight blue from designer Bill Levkoff. The bridesmaid with perfectly chiseled arms may choose the spaghetti-strap number, while the bride with the impressive décolletage may choose the dress with the plunging neckline. Because they're all in the same color, this option offers uniformity as well as a sense of individual style. It also allows bridesmaids to choose a dress that's personally flattering and comfortable. These dresses may also come with additional options such as shawls or jackets, for bridesmaids who wish to cover up a bit more.

QUESTION?

What should I do with the bridesmaid dress after I've worn it?

Wear it again, if you're lucky enough to like it. Or take it to a consignment shop—you can often bring in a decent percentage paid by reselling it.

Who Chooses?

So what's ultimately the process in choosing a dress? And how can you encourage your bride to choose attire with options? Again, every bride is different. Some brides will take along all their bridesmaids to choose a dress, though this method may be a bit daunting. The probability that five or more women would settle upon one dress and color in a single shopping trip seems near impossible.

More likely, the bride will shop with her maid of honor or mother to narrow down the choices and colors; then, she may solicit the opinions of all her bridesmaids. Or she may simply decide upon one dress unilaterally, informing you later about her choice. The considerate bride will have kept everyone's interests in mind–including everyone's shape, size, and personal style–in order to choose a dress that all her bridesmaids will at least feel comfortable wearing.

The Lowdown on Styles

So what are some of the more popular styles? Bridesmaid dresses–as most dresses–will differ by length, silhouette, and fabric. The following are some of the more popular choices in each of these categories.

Length

- **Floor length.** This is the most popular length among bridesmaid dresses. As the name implies, this dress will fall approximately one inch from the floor.
- **Ankle length.** A bit shorter than floor length, this style just shows the ankles.
- **Tea length.** Shorter still than ankle length, tea length falls just at the mid-shin, or a bit below.

Silhouette

- **Ball gown.** Think Cinderella. Ball gowns are characterized by a tight, fitted bodice and a very full skirt, with a fitted, defined waistline.
- **A-line.** This is an extremely popular style among bridesmaid dresses, as it fits many body types comfortably. This dress has two vertical seams that start at the shoulders, flaring with an "A" shape to the floor. The dress typically skims the body without fitting snugly in any one location.

- **Empire.** Also called "empire waist." This dress is defined by its very high waistline, which falls right under the bust. The skirt falls from there, and is usually straight and fairly slim.
- **Sheath.** Tight and fitted from top to bottom, this dress may flare near the ankles.

FACT

For fun, after the wedding's over, have a hideous bridesmaid dress party. Invite all your girlfriends to come wearing their least favorite bridesmaid dress and swap stories about weddings past.

Fabrics

- **Linen.** A popular fabric for spring and summer bridesmaid dresses, this is a lightweight fabric that wrinkles easily.
- **Satin.** This is a year-round bridesmaid dress fabric, also very popular. It's smooth with a high sheen, and cool to the touch.
- **Silk.** This strong fabric only looks delicate. It is also smooth and sometimes has a sheen. It is traditionally quite expensive.
- **Chiffon.** Sheer, largely transparent material that is often used in layers. It creates a very soft, feminine effect in dresses.
- **Taffeta.** A stiffer fabric, with a small, crisscross rib; smooth and usually shiny like satin.

- **Brocade.** A heavier fabric that is usually woven with an intricate design.

Occasionally, a bride will allow her bridesmaids to choose their own destiny by shopping for their own dresses. She may give you one simple parameter, such as color or length, or she may let you have completely free reign. And while this is every bridesmaid's dream, it is also quite rare. If you are lucky enough to choose your own dress, you will obviously be able to pick something that's flattering and in your specific price range–always a welcome opportunity.

Chapter 4

Always a Bridesmaid . . .

There are countless special circumstances that may come to light when serving as a bridesmaid. Usually your good judgment will guide you, but from time to time you may feel a bit stymied, unsure of how to proceed. This chapter gives you some guidance by anticipating a number of common scenarios you may encounter—with advice on how best to deal with them. All this while maintaining the highest possible level of diplomacy along the way, without compromising yourself in the process.

The Pregnant Bridesmaid

So the bride has asked you to be a bridesmaid, and you're already pregnant. Or, you become pregnant partway through your bridesmaid stint. Congratulations on the exciting news! But how, if at all, will your pregnancy affect the wedding and your role as bridesmaid?

As with everything else in your life, being pregnant shouldn't make that much of an impact. You can work, you can exercise, so you can certainly serve as a bridesmaid. It's when the children are actually born that things really change.

Unfortunately, this may come as a surprise to some brides. In fact, a recent visit to a wedding-related message board on the Internet yielded some surprising chatter for a supposedly enlightened day and age. One message posting was from a bride in Tulsa, who was seeking advice regarding what to do about her pregnant bridesmaid–should she ask her to "step down" from the bridal party? Unbelievably, she elicited the sympathy of more than one fellow bride, who responded that yes indeed, she should feel no remorse in asking a bridesmaid who'd become pregnant to respectfully give up her duties. Their reasoning, mainly, revolved around the pregnant bridesmaid "throwing off the pictures" and "standing out too much from the other bridesmaids."

If you suspect you're dealing with a bride who has similar views, know you have the sympathy of (most of) womankind, despite these few Bridezillas (more on her later in this chapter). If the situation arises–you become pregnant and the bride expresses that she'd rather you didn't participate any longer (and you suspect her reasons are entirely shallow)–accept her wishes gracefully. Then run like mad. This woman is not your friend, and you're better off realizing this now than later. She didn't deserve your commitment to this role in the first place. A bride who cares more for the aesthetics of her wedding day than she does about being surrounded by close friends and family is truly selfish and self-centered.

ESSENTIAL

So you're pregnant. You're still going to work, still exercising—there's no reason you can't still be a bridesmaid. Embrace and enjoy it—at least you'll stand out from the other bridesmaids.

On the other hand, there may be some circumstances when the bride may be acting altruistically. Maybe you've had a difficult pregnancy, have been ill, or are stressed out. There is a chance she's trying to let you off easy, so she doesn't add more stress to your load. If you suspect this is her motive–or you're not entirely sure–have an open talk with her. As with any conflict or misunderstanding, it's the only way you'll get honest answers.

Bad Timing

The only pregnancy issue that might legitimately affect your serving out your duties is timing. Obviously, if your due date falls on the same day as the wedding, you may have a problem. If the wedding is out of town, for instance, your doctor may advise against traveling for two weeks to a month before your due date (if travel involves flying). That will prevent you from walking down that aisle, whether you want to or not. So what should you do?

If you know that you're pregnant when you're asked to be a bridesmaid, let the bride know as soon as possible. If you haven't told anyone yet, then tell her as soon as you officially announce it. Unless it's a travel issue or a conflicting due date, it shouldn't make a difference.

FACT

Here's some proof that way-pregnant women can do it all: Catherine Zeta-Jones at the 2003 Academy Awards. Not only did she look amazing accepting the Best Supporting Actress Oscar just weeks before she was due, but she also performed a song from her movie *Chicago,* live onstage.

If it *is* an issue of bad timing, but the wedding is in or around your hometown, the issue is a bit trickier. Suppose your due date is very close to the wedding date. You'll be on the brink of giving birth when the wedding takes place. There's a good chance you won't be feeling up to the stress of a wedding this close to your due date. And it would be a shame if you invested in a dress, shoes, and accessories only to give birth two days before the wedding and miss the whole thing.

If the wedding is a few hours away, you may also be hesitant to stray too far from your doctor or hospital. Special circumstances like these require careful deliberation. Talk to the bride and make her aware of the situation. If you simply know you won't feel up to it, most brides will find a very late-term pregnancy a perfectly legitimate excuse to decline.

The Dress

Luckily, you're not the first pregnant woman to serve as a bridesmaid–nor will you be the last. Most bridal salons and bridesmaid dress shops offer expert advice on the best styles for a pregnant bridesmaid, as well as expertise on predicting what your correct size will be at the time of the wedding.

Obviously, you may not be able to dictate the dress style–the bride may have already done that–but if you have some say, or if the bride is allowing you to choose your own style, an empire-waist dress is probably your best bet. This style dress, which has a skirt that falls from immediately below the bust line, will allow plenty of room for a growing belly to fit comfortably.

Other styles, such as an A-line, will also work. For any style that isn't a maternity cut, you'll need to order a much larger size to accommodate your belly, then have the bust and shoulders of the dress taken in by a seamstress or tailor.

You may also suggest to the bride that you have your dress custom-made, using the same fabric and color chosen for the rest of the bridesmaid dresses. This way you can more easily gauge the correct size (you won't have to guesstimate what you'll look like six months in advance if you have the dress made a few weeks before the wedding), and you'll have a dress specifically designed for maternity wear. That means there's space for the belly, but the rest of the dress will fit normally, unlike a non-maternity bridesmaid dress, which will be too big in the bust, shoulders, and hips because you've ordered a significantly larger size.

ALERT!

If you're pregnant, be sure to solicit advice from the consultants at the dress shop before ordering your dress. They have the experience to predict what size you'll need five months from now.

This was the case with one pregnant New York City bridesmaid. Normally a size four, she was advised to order a size fourteen to accommodate her swelling belly. When she got it, the dress fit perfectly in the midsection, but resembled a tent everywhere else—and alterations didn't help much. So she had a dress in the same color and fabric custom-made in a maternity style, and ended up with a much more comfortable—and flattering–alternative. Of course, your best bet is to convince the bride of this option before you end up paying for two dresses. She shouldn't mind, as long as you don't stray too far from the chosen style.

The Newly Engaged Bridesmaid

So you're a bridesmaid . . . and also a bride-to-be! Congratulations. This is one wedding season you won't soon forget.

Certainly, the fact that you've become engaged shouldn't affect serving out your role as bridesmaid. However, life can become stressful and overwhelming when trying to plan your own wedding's events–not to mention juggling shower plans, bachelorette party plans, and dress fittings for the other bride in your life, too. If this describes your situation, stop and take a deep breath–and get organized. As with any other life situation, a wise use of your time will be your greatest asset when balancing all your responsibilities.

Be careful to avoid the most obvious pitfall–neglecting your bridesmaid duties now that you're a bride-to-be. It's easily done, in the face of all the other details you need to arrange–but you don't want to let the bride down, or the other bridesmaids. After all, now that you're a bride yourself you can appreciate the value of everyone's enthusiastic participation, right?

When planning your own wedding, you should also avoid eclipsing your friend's/sister's/cousin's plans with your own. That means you should avoid setting your own wedding date to fall, say, a week before her wedding. Refrain from choosing a similar dress or one the exact same color, and don't plan your wedding to be held at the exact same wedding location.

ESSENTIAL

If you're serving as bridesmaid and planning your own wedding at the same time, be sure not to neglect your bridesmaid duties. Just as you're counting on your own bridesmaids, the other bride is counting on you.

These actions would inevitably be viewed with great annoyance. In addition, consider the dates of the other bride's shower(s), bachelorette party, and other preparties when finalizing the dates for your own soirees.

So Many Brides, So Little Time . . .

For years, your group of girls reveled in swinging singleness, enjoying weekly outings to new clubs and restaurants, taking pottery classes, complaining about loser guys. Then poof! Everyone's suddenly engaged. Not only that, but their wedding dates all fall within weeks of each other. And between your friends, your family, and your boyfriend's friends and family, you've even been invited to multiple weddings on the same day! What's a good friend to do?

This is a dilemma you will inevitably encounter at some point in your young life. It's like an extension of the synchronized "monthly cycle" phenomenon–turns out that groups of women also conform to the same nuptial cycle. Call it pheromones, call it aggressive husband-hunting–but once the first domino falls, the rest seem to follow. Unfortunately, this phenomenon will end up adversely affecting *you.* Because, after all, you can't be two places at one time. So how do you prioritize which weddings you'll attend?

Double Duty

If you've been asked to be a bridesmaid in any of these weddings, they should take immediate priority over the weddings at which you'll be a regular guest. In other words, if you're invited to two weddings in the same weekend, and in one of these you've been asked to be a bridesmaid, it's clear which one you'll need to attend. Sure, you'll be bummed to miss the other wedding, but you're an honored guest at this one, and that comes first.

But what if you're asked to be a bridesmaid in two weddings on the same day? Seem impossible? Unfortunately, it's been known to happen. For this scenario, you'll have to do some serious soul-searching, like the Baltimore bridesmaid who faced this very same dilemma. As much as it pained her, she had to choose to be a bridesmaid for one of two of her friends' weddings, as one wedding was in Pittsburgh and the other in Cleveland.

Choosing between friends is never easy, and it was even harder to break the news to the bride whose wedding she wouldn't be attending. But to make up for her absence at the wedding, this bridesmaid made a valiant effort to travel to town before the wedding, attending the bridal shower and bachelorette party. Because of her honesty and efforts, she and the bride remain close, and there are no hard feelings.

QUESTION?

What's proper etiquette if I'm invited to two weddings in one day?
Some say you should attend the wedding whose invitation you received first. Others say to choose the event of the person you're closer with. If you can, make an appearance at both; if not, use your good judgment to make your decision.

If you face a situation like this, honesty is the best policy. Even if you can't be at one of the weddings, you can fulfill your prewedding bridesmaid responsibilities, like helping to throw a shower or assisting in the wedding plans. In the end, being a good friend will always override bad circumstances—or unfortunate coincidences.

The Overly Popular Bridesmaid

Of course, being asked to be a bridesmaid in more than one wedding can cause some fallout, even if the weddings *don't* fall on the same day. As you've learned, being in one wedding is an expense—two or three in a single season might be more than you can (financially) bear. What to do?

If you have enough notice, your first strategy is to begin saving early. Put away a specific amount of money each month to ensure you'll have the proper funds when the day comes. That means figuring in the cost of the dress, showers, bachelorette parties, and travel expenses.

Putting some of these expenses onto a credit card is also an option, though not highly recommended—you'll end up paying a ridiculous amount of interest for the privilege of using the money now. And it seems downright silly to go into serious debt for a few bridesmaid dresses. A better bet might be a no- or low-interest loan from your parents, if they're willing and able to provide it.

FACT

It's not uncommon to serve as bridesmaid multiple times within a short time span. And while it may get a bit expensive, remember that it's an honor that you've been included in your friends' or family members' once-in-a-lifetime event.

If you truly know you cannot afford to be in all of these bridal parties, though, simply let the brides know. Once again, you may need to choose between brides, and this may be an extremely difficult decision. Let your heart and conscience guide you through. If it's very important to the bride, perhaps she'll offer to subsidize some of your expenses or to give you an alternative honored role, such as doing a wedding-day reading. That way you can still be part of the festivities but without the financial obligation.

Confronting Your Inner Bride

The most challenging circumstances when serving as bridesmaid are often, actually, your complete *lack* of circumstances—namely, you're quite single and not all that happy about it.

Being Single

Maybe you've just ended a long-term relationship. Maybe you're in the middle of a dry spell—whatever the situation, you feel as if it's a couple's world and you're not part of it. Being a bridesmaid in a close friend's or family member's wedding only makes your situation that much more pronounced. And all this talk about love, commitment, and finding the "one" would eat a hole in anyone's fragile psyche.

So how do you handle a situation when you feel as if the old cliché was written just for you—"Always a bridesmaid, never a bride"? First of all, let's put things into perspective. Life is never perfect for everyone at any one time. The bride probably went through a bad spell or two of her own—her timing is simply "on" right now.

At the risk of sounding like your mother or grandmother, your day *will* come. And when it does, these feelings will all be just a dim memory. In fact, in ten years, when you're comfortably married with a tyke or two, you may find yourself longing for the very days when you were single and believed you were so miserable. Life's funny that way.

Still Dating

Maybe your "always a bridesmaid" status has a slightly different twist, however. Maybe you're not single at all. Maybe you've been dating the same guy for quite a long time, and you've watched as girlfriend after girlfriend has gotten engaged before you. When will your time come? Should you dump your boyfriend after all the time you've invested? Should you give him an ultimatum?

Unfortunately, your friend's circumstances can force long-latent issues like this one to the surface. Because when your sister and your best friend are planning their weddings, it's difficult not to imagine yourself in a similar situation–and to start questioning the circumstances in your own life.

Don't dump your boyfriend. And DON'T give him an ultimatum. Rather, give yourself some time to determine what's causing your anxiety. Is it the wedding hoopla that's making you crazy, or are your anxieties based in reality? Is marriage something you really want with this person? Or do you just long to plan a wedding and reap all the attention that comes with it? Sometimes, in the frenzy of planning a friend's wedding, these feelings can become confused. Then again, sometimes they're a totally legitimate wake-up call.

ALERT!

Difficult as it may be as a bridesmaid, try not to let wedding fever overcome you. It's natural to imagine yourself in the bride's position, but don't let it affect your self-esteem or your own romantic relationship.

Attitude Matters

Regardless of your conclusions, do all you can *not* to make this wedding about you. Show enthusiasm and commitment as a bridesmaid for your friend or family member's wedding, and put your all into making this the best wedding it can be. The consideration you show will come back in spades when it's finally your time to wed.

A bad attitude—or a perceived bad attitude—can unfortunately be a friendship-breaker. Take Cynthia and Stacey, two women who became best friends in college. They were always a bit competitive, and their mutual friends knew trouble would begin brewing as soon as Cynthia announced she was engaged. Cynthia asked Stacey to be a bridesmaid, but despite this fact they grew distant during the engagement.

Cynthia contended that the boyfriend-free Stacey resented the fact that she was happily engaged, while

Stacey felt that Cynthia had become completely self-absorbed and obsessed with her wedding–to the exclusion of everything and everyone else. Unfortunately, they never voiced these feelings to each other, which festered and grew to ungainly proportions. And the friendship ultimately didn't survive it.

The point? Feelings of envy are a normal part of life. But letting these feelings control and ruin a perfectly good friendship is unnecessary and immature. You should never allow someone's good fortune to throw a dark shadow on a friendship. However, if you sense your feelings of envy are getting *out* of control–causing you outright depression or anger–it may be time to get some additional help. Try talking to a trusted friend, clergy member, or a therapist for objective advice. There's no sense in suffering when help is readily available.

Taming Bridezilla

Of course, bridesmaid Stacey, even if she was a tad resentful, may have also had a point. The most well-meaning brides often turn beast-like when it comes to planning their weddings. What are the roots of this phenomenon?

In most cases, it starts with the pursuit of perfection. Combine it with a little competition. Add a dash of utter fantasy, along with a sprinkle of obliviousness, and you'll have the makings of Bridezilla–the seemingly normal woman who goes, well, ballistic during her engagement.

Who Is She?

Bridezilla is the woman who's going into deep debt to throw her wedding. Or the woman who's thrown multiple tantrums to get her way with her parents. She's the bride who's put years of thought into her wedding day, but barely minutes into the days and years that will follow it. She's the bride who's alienating her parents, in-laws, fiancé, and other interested parties because there's only one way to throw this wedding–her way. She's probably the bride fighting with her mother, her future mother-in-law, or her fiancé as you read this sentence.

ESSENTIAL

Don't accept Bridezilla's abuse just because you're her bridesmaid. If her behavior violates the normal code of friendship, it's unacceptable during her engagement as well. Remember—you're her bridesmaid, not her hired lackey.

There's been more attention paid to Bridezilla in recent years, as her behavior becomes more subject to scrutiny. Society has long accepted the notion of the blushing bride playing princess for a day. And the wedding industry has perpetuated this fantasy, promoting a no-holds-barred expectation when it comes to spending time, money, and resources in pursuit of this "dream." This pressure has had dire results on some brides in recent years, who will often go to extreme measures to ensure it happens. Like spending money they don't have. Demanding things no rational woman would demand. And thinking about the wedding day more than their impending marriages.

FACT

Perhaps your Bridezilla is normally a sane, rational girl. As her good friend, it may be necessary to call her out on her dreadful behavior, especially if it's beginning to affect her relationships with others.

Is This Normal?

Now, it's important to draw a distinction between the normal, enthusiastic bride and Bridezilla. Planning any kind of wedding comes with a certain amount of stress and pressure. It also breeds excitement about seemingly minute details, like napkin colors and pew bows. Add this planning stress and excitement to work and family responsibilities, and it's normal for any bride to experience highs and lows–including moments when she's frustrated, stressed out, depressed, or simply numb.

You'll find Bridezilla, however, in a stratosphere beyond the normal bride. That's because Bridezilla often *creates* stress for herself and for those around her, with demands and expectations that go beyond the norm. That's where her wrath can end up affecting you, as her bridesmaid. How, you ask? Take the case of Martha and Kim as an example, a bride and bridesmaid from Dallas.

Martha, the bride, has never been a stranger from attention. As an only child, her parents doted on her from childhood, both emotionally and financially. As a teenager, she was a real live debutante. When it came time to plan her wedding, it was no surprise that she and her family would put on quite an extravaganza. What did come as a surprise, however, was how she treated her bridesmaids.

Martha and Kim had been friends for eight years—since their freshman year in college. Martha had always been a good and loyal friend, and though they'd been brought up very differently, they had a great relationship.

But during the wedding planning, Martha began treating Kim more like her hired assistant than as a trusted confidante. She demanded that all her bridesmaids buy very expensive dresses, jewelry, and shoes (with shoes alone costing almost $200). She had Kim running wedding-related errands for her three to four times per week. One Friday, Martha called Kim to tell her a mutual friend was coming in for the weekend, and that she'd be dropping her off to stay at Kim's house—Martha and her fiancé had decided to take a last-minute trip to Vegas.

Kim was a good sport about all of these things, if sometimes annoyed at Martha's lack of common courtesy. But when Martha mentioned to Kim that she'd look a lot better as a bridesmaid if she "took off a few pounds," that was the last straw. Kim confronted Martha and told her while she was happy to be a bridesmaid and to help Martha where she could, she wasn't going to take her abuse any longer.

Out of Control

The bottom line is that being a bridesmaid shouldn't become a daily obligation. It shouldn't give the bride license to act in ways that would normally be judged as rude or inconsiderate, just because her actions are wedding-related. Being a bridesmaid should always abide by the "girl code," long established among your friends and/or family members.

ALERT!

Don't confuse Bridezilla with the actions of a rational bride. As a bridesmaid it is your duty to help the bride with wedding-related tasks; it's when she crosses the line and you begin suffering for the sake of her wedding that her behavior becomes unacceptable.

And the bride should never make requests that cause her bridesmaids to feel uncomfortable or pressured to do something they wouldn't normally do. Like the Jacksonville, Florida, bride who asked all her bridesmaids to get identical, chin-length bobs a few weeks before the wedding. Or the bride in Mobile, Alabama, with the all-blonde bridal party—except for one. She actually asked the chestnut-hued brunette to dye her hair blonde for the wedding, so all the girls would "match."

If the actions of these brides sound familiar, you have our sympathy. It's not easy dealing with a woman whose wedding has given her carte blanche in the manners department. But besides commiserating with other friends and family members about her audacity, is there anything else you can do?

What Should You Do?

Remember, being a bridesmaid is always voluntary. Hard as it may be, there may be circumstances that justify dropping out of the bridal party. Before you do, though, be sure to communicate your feelings with the bride. There's a chance she may not even realize she's been behaving badly, and if she's reasonable she'll try to correct her actions rather than lose a bridesmaid—or a friend.

If you suspect she'll never see the error of her ways, though, try this approach. Tell her that under the present circumstances you're unable to serve as a supportive, enthusiastic bridesmaid, so you'd rather not be a hypocrite and continue on. Without accusing her outright, this will get your point across that she's acting like a complete ninny. And perhaps it will prompt her to engage in a little self-reflection.

Girl Trouble

Bridezilla? No way. You've got the bride from heaven . . . it's the bridesmaids from hell who are causing you angst. Who are these chicks, anyway?

Get almost any group of people together to complete a task, and there's bound to be some conflict. Like every office breeds politics, and every sorority breeds enmity, every bridal party has its touchy moments. Tina's not pitching in enough. Jackie's trying to control everyone. Maura's lazy. Angela thinks she's all that.

So how do you promote diplomacy among a group of women who may or may not know each other? The answer is patience. Although it's the maid of honor who finds herself in the hot seat when it comes to directing and organizing the group, as a bridesmaid, you can also be an ambassador of goodwill among the girls. Miss Nuptial Congeniality, so to speak.

If you're planning a shower and/or bachelorette party, any number of scenarios may arise among your group. The following outline some of the more common ones, with quick solutions that can smooth things over for the whole bridal party–including the bride, who should never be burdened with the prospect of feuding bridesmaids.

The Indifferent Bridesmaid

This girl doesn't take the initiative on anything. While the rest of the bridesmaids snap up tasks like making shower decorations, taking on cooking duties, or organizing games, this bridesmaid hasn't volunteered once to help out.

Solution: Delegate tasks to her. She may not even realize she's slacking; some people simply need to be told what to do. Rather than resenting her, simply get her involved–and then get over it.

The Take-Control Bridesmaid

The maid of honor's supposed to be running the show. But this bridesmaid is making independent moves with shower and bachelorette party plans–and demanding the rest of the girls' help. Who should you be listening to?

Solution: Hold a bridesmaid pow-wow. The maid of honor should ultimately be calling the shots, but perhaps she's delegated some tasks to this bridesmaid and you were simply unaware. Or maybe your initial impression is correct, and this busybody is just a rogue bridesmaid acting inappropriately. There's only one way to find out. Meet, and bring up plans among the group. When they're brought to the light of day with everyone in attendance, plans will inevitably get ironed out, and everyone will have a say.

 **FACT**

Bridesmaids should work as a team to complete tasks such as shower and bachelorette party planning. No one bridesmaid (with the exception of the maid of honor) should have to handle the brunt of the responsibility.

The Troubled Bridesmaid

Perhaps she's gotten into some financial trouble. Or she's having some problems with drinking and/or drugs. Or maybe she's simply going through a bout of depression. No matter what the problem, being a bridesmaid has not been high on her list of priorities.

Solution: Be a friend. Try to help her with the root cause of her problem, if possible, or to steer her toward someone who can help. And try not to attack her for shirking her bridesmaid duties, even if it means taking up some of the slack yourself. Being put on the defensive by you or the other bridesmaids may only add to her current burden.

The Absent Bridesmaid

This bridesmaid is a regular no-show for parties, showers, and other wedding-related events. You know that her behavior has been hurtful and disappointing to the bride. Is there anything you should do?

Solution: Use your judgment. If you think a few well-chosen, nonconfrontational words will affect this bridesmaid's behavior, then offer them. If you know that talking to her will do no good, though, don't get involved. It may only cause more problems and tension for the bride in the long run.

The Bitchy Bridesmaid

You've just met her, and already you can't stand her. Or you've known her forever and you can stand her even less. She's selfish and snobbish, and frankly you can't even believe the bride's still friends with her.

Solution: There is none. Unfortunately, there are plenty of unpleasant people we have to deal with in life, and it's not up to you to change this woman's personality. Try to put up with her no matter how you feel about her, for the sake of the bride. After all, the bride shouldn't have to deal with bridesmaid conflict, along with everything else she's juggling right now.

If possible, give this bridesmaid the benefit of the doubt. Maybe it's simply a long history of disdain and indifference toward each other that's affecting your attitudes. After all, you do have the bride in common. Give her one more chance, and see whether she'll warm up—maybe she's simply been on the defensive all this time.

The Broke Bridesmaid

She's constantly complaining about money. And no matter how budget-conscious you all are while planning the shower and bachelorette party, she's still singing the blues about her contribution.

Solution: Perhaps she really is in bad financial straits. Or maybe she's just cheap. If you know her at all, you've probably got a good gauge on the situation. If she really is having some problems, try to give her a break. Get together with the rest of the bridesmaids and see if you can cover her share, or plan a less extravagant event. If you suspect she's just being tight with her money, compromise on the cost of the affair—then be firm about her contribution. You're all in this together.

Chapter 5

Fun, Fabulous Showers

One of your most important duties as a bridesmaid is to help plan a shower for the bride. Showers can vary a great deal in size and style, and in recent years they've become more and more creative—no longer always the traditional, somewhat formal, women-only gatherings they once were. Today's showers may include guests numbering from 10 to 100, they may be held on a weekend or a weeknight, and they may even include—gasp!—men as guests.

What's the Point?

The main objective of the shower is to help furnish the bride (and groom) with the household items they'll need to start making a home. Traditionally, showers have been weekend afternoon gatherings of women only, with food, games, activities, and gift-giving.

But today's showers are more open to interpretation. Bridesmaids and family members are hosting different kinds of gatherings that incorporate creative activities, unique foods and cocktails, and fun new games. For the bridesmaid, today's looser interpretation of showers can both complicate and ease your planning duties. The one thing all showers should have in common, however, is that they serve a practical purpose—gifts for the bride—as well as providing a forum to celebrate the upcoming nuptials.

This chapter helps you narrow down your options, choosing the best style and size shower to suit your bride—as well as your budget. It offers ideas for specific themes, along with ideas for shower games, activities, and creative gifts. It also gives you a step-by-step look at precisely what needs to be planned and who needs to plan it.

So read ahead, get organized, and get ready to have some fun.

History of the Shower

It's said that the first shower was held in Holland hundreds of years ago. A Dutch woman fell in love with a poor miller who had become impoverished by generously giving away his goods and money to those in need. Her father did not approve of this marriage, which he felt was beneath her, preferring she marry a wealthier man whom his daughter did not love.

He tried to get his way by refusing to give a dowry to the poor miller, knowing the two would not have the means to establish a home. When the townspeople heard of the couple's fate, they decided to take matters into their own hands, "showering" the couple with the household items they needed to make a start, thus repaying the miller's longtime generosity.

Legend also has it that it was an Englishwoman who brought the concept of a shower into the modern age. Wishing she could give a friend a more substantial engagement gift, but without the means to do so, she decided to throw a party at which everyone could present their gifts at once. This way, the bride would be showered with many gifts, not just the woman's humble offering.

Defining Your Options

No matter what the genesis, over the past fifty-plus years, showers have followed certain traditions and patterns that haven't varied a whole lot. These showers traditionally included these characteristics:

- Women only
- Held on a weekend morning or afternoon

- A light lunch and dessert
- Ice-breaker games and/or activities
- Small gifts or favors for the guests
- Focused upon the bride opening her gifts

Shower Alternatives

The traditional shower standard, while enjoyable for many, doesn't suit every bride. For instance, some brides may not want to receive gifts at all. Some may prefer a male/female guest list, and some may hate the idea of playing games. And while it's easy to go with the traditional shower format outlined here, you may also wish to determine if your bride would take exception to some of these traditions—or if she would simply enjoy, or be more comfortable with, some new traditions.

ESSENTIAL

Follow the bride's personality as a guide to the type of shower you'll host. Feel free to break certain traditions if they don't fit with her tastes or expectations. For example, she may prefer a coed or a no-gifts shower, both of which veer from tradition.

What's Your Shower Style?

The following questions will get you thinking about the bride's personality and interests. You may also wish to talk to the bride directly to learn her preferences—

she may have her heart set on some specific shower ideas, for example, or she may know she doesn't want to include others. Or, if the shower's a surprise, you can use the following questions and answers to get some insight into what would make her happiest:

- Does the bride's close social circle include male as well as female acquaintances?
- Does the bride prefer girls-only or mixed gatherings?
- Does attention and fuss make the bride uncomfortable?
- Is the bride typically more laid-back and casual or more high maintenance?
- Is the bride very picky about what she eats and drinks?
- Does the bride like large, boisterous groups, or is she more comfortable among a small group of intimates?
- Are there a lot of bridesmaids, or just a few? (It's typically the case that the more bridesmaids, the larger the shower.)
- Which better represents the bride—Chardonnay and crudités, or beer and burgers?
- Is the bride a stickler for etiquette?

The answers to these questions will obviously go a long way in determining what style shower she'd most enjoy. For instance, if the bride has as many male friends as female, she may really appreciate a coed shower. If she's a beer and burgers gal, she'll probably be more comfortable with a laid-back, casual shower than an English tea. And if she likes doing things by the book, she probably won't feel right about a shower with a wacky theme or unusual activities. So use your answers to these questions—and your instinct—to plan a shower that the bride and everyone else will enjoy.

Planning Checklist

Before you even begin determining the style or planning the specific shower details, it will help to know exactly what elements you'll need to think about when planning any type of shower. The following checklist is meant to help you organize your thoughts, as well as the details, as you begin the planning process.

Venue

- ❒ Home
- ❒ Restaurant
- ❒ Country club
- ❒ Banquet facility
- ❒ Outdoors
- ❒ Other: ______________________

Guest List

- ❒ Family members
- ❒ Friends
- ❒ Bridal party
- ❒ Men
- ❒ Children

Food

❒ Lunch

❒ Brunch

❒ Dinner

❒ Hors d'oeuvres only

❒ Cake and sweets only

Drinks

❒ Non-alcoholic only

❒ Punch

❒ Wine

❒ Martinis

❒ Cocktails

❒ Beer

Decorations

❒ Flowers

❒ Balloons

❒ Linens

❒ China

❒ Silver

❒ Other: ______________________________

Favors/Prizes

____

Games

____

Activities

____

____

Setting the Tone

Filling in the blanks for the checklist is your next step. The great thing is that there are so many options. The difficult thing is narrowing those options down to just a few. Clearly, some of these options are limited by your budget and by your capabilities. For example, don't plan to serve a formal lunch for twenty at your home if you're helpless in the kitchen (unless you have it catered).

FACT

A bridal shower should be held one to two months before the wedding date. Avoid scheduling it too close to the wedding, as this is an extremely busy time. Be sure to consult with the bride (and her mother) before making the date official.

And you'd be wise to narrow down the guest list—or serve a limited menu—if you've got a very small budget. These points are fairly obvious, but in the frenzy and expectations wrought by the engagement period, they are sometimes overlooked in favor of throwing a "fantasy" party. Here's some good advice: Be realistic when planning this shindig, or you'll probably be very disappointed.

The Guest List

Before you even begin to plan your party's particulars, you should probably determine the guest list. Many factors contribute to developing the guest list, but the bride and her family should ultimately finalize this list.

But if you and the bridesmaids are throwing the party, shouldn't you be able to invite anyone you want? Yes, and no. The first rule of thumb when throwing any shower is to invite only people who will also be invited to the wedding. You should never invite guests who will not make the final wedding invitation list. They will feel as if they were only invited to the shower for their ability to proffer a gift, which is really not far off the mark.

Typically, you need not (and should not) include all the female names on the wedding guest list—only close friends and family members should be invited. The average size for a shower is ten to twenty guests, though obviously showers can be and are often much larger. It's probably best to work with the bride or her mother to develop an appropriate list.

The next step to help narrow down your list is to determine if the bride will be having any other showers. For example, if her aunts are throwing her a big, catered affair for fifty, then you may wish to plan a much smaller gathering of close friends and immediate family only. In other words, if the aunts have all the extended female relatives on the bride's and groom's sides covered, then it's perfectly okay to host a smaller, more intimate shower.

If yours will be the bride's only shower, however, you'll probably wish to open it up to friends and family members of the bride and groom, so everyone can meet, greet, and celebrate in advance of the wedding.

Of course, you may also decide to have a coed, or couples, shower. Because this will immediately double the size of your party, your best bet is to invite the bride's and groom's immediate family only, along with perhaps a few close friends. Or keep it among your contemporaries only and just invite the bride and groom's immediate social circle, including the bridesmaids and groomsmen. You may also wish to include the bride's and groom's parents, so they can meet or mingle with everyone before the festivities.

FACT

Coed, or "couples," showers are growing in popularity, allowing both male and female friends and family to celebrate together before the wedding. A couples shower can be an especially good alternative if there was no engagement party.

Of course, the entire bridal party should be invited to every shower, as should the bride's mother (and her sisters, if they are not already bridesmaids). The bridal party is also expected to attend every prewedding event–which includes showers. So even if you're helping host one of the showers, you still need to attend the other three.

Excluding a "problem" guest will always cause more grief than including her. If there's someone you don't particularly care for, remember—err on the side of caution. This is not the time to create new problems.

Shower Themes

One of the decisions that will drive the remaining planning details is whether or not to throw a theme shower.

What is a theme shower, you ask? It's anything with an overriding concept or idea attached to it, beyond the expected shower activities. For example, at a gourmet shower, the guests give kitchen or food-related gifts. You'd serve gourmet goodies, and you might feature an activity like a professional cooking lesson for all the attendees.

But a theme shower needn't be complicated or involve special activities–you can fashion a theme around all the traditional shower activities, with a slight twist. For example, you could throw a shower whose theme is gift-related only, like a round-the-clock shower. For this type of shower, each guest is assigned a different time of day; the gift they bring should correspond to that time of day. For example, a time of 11 P.M. might inspire a gift of lingerie–or a SnackMaster. A time of 7 A.M. might inspire a coffee-maker, a hair dryer, or an electric toothbrush.

You can limit this type of theme just to gifts, or you can expand it with decorations, favors, and food, too, if the spirit moves you. For example, you might give each guest a small clock or a calendar as favors; you might serve a cake that's been decorated to resemble a clock; or you might give the bride a "countdown" clock that counts the hours and minutes until her wedding day.

QUESTION?

As a bridesmaid, if I attend three showers, do I have to give three gifts?
Etiquette advises that no, you do not. But you may wish to consider giving one substantial gift, followed by two smaller gifts, so you won't feel as though you're arriving empty-handed at any of the events.

There are countless other themes you can incorporate into your celebration. Read ahead to find one that's perfect for your get-together.

ABC Shower

At this shower, each guest is assigned a letter of the alphabet, and her gift should reflect that letter. For example, if she's assigned the letter "c," she might give the bride a clock, or a Cuisinart, or a Calphalon pan. The fun behind the alphabet shower lies in the creative lengths that guests will go to in fulfilling their assigned letter. Again, you can tie the theme into any other aspect of the shower, such as games, food, or decorations. Serve alphabet soup. Give guests favors like magnetic poetry sets or bookmarks.

Fitness Shower

So the bride's an outdoorswoman or a sports buff. You know that she'd appreciate a new set of ski bindings ten times more than a new blender. There's just one thing to do—hold a fitness shower!

For this theme, be sure to give guests some guidance as to appropriate gifts. While most women have some insight in choosing glassware, many women won't have the first clue about choosing the right thermal wear. If possible, have the bride register for sports-related gifts at an all-purpose sports store, like Sports Authority. If no store near you offers a formal registry service, see if they'll design a makeshift one for the special occasion. A privately owned local sports store might be more inclined to help out this way.

If you know that many of the guests are also sports-minded, incorporate some fitness-related activities into the shower. Take a hike, a bike ride, or play tennis with the group. Give nonsporting guests an alternative, such as arriving for food, drinks, and gift-giving afterward, or include them as drivers or spectators so no one feels left out.

Hobby Shower

This theme is perfect for the bride with lots of interests. It's also ideal for the bride and groom who've been on their own for a while and don't need to be set up with home essentials like towels, sheets, and cookware.

The hobby shower is meant to encourage gift-giving related to the bride's favorite activities. For example, maybe she loves to read, or she's totally into scrapbooking, and she can't get enough yoga. Appropriate gifts in this case might include a reading lamp, a beautiful bookmark, a yoga membership, a yoga mat, fitness clothing, or scrapbooking accessories. In case guests aren't specifically aware, let them know the bride's interests on the invitation. Of course, the theme can also be extended to the groom's hobbies, too.

Once again, any of the hobbies can be incorporated into the shower activities, as well. You might all have a scrapbooking session, or you can pay a yoga instructor to make a house call to your shower. As with anything, give guests who choose not, or are unable to engage in the activity, an option to do something else.

ESSENTIAL

As the bride opens her gifts, be sure you or another bridesmaid is recording every detail. List each specific gift with a detailed description, along with the corresponding gift-giver. This will ensure the bride has the correct information when she writes thank-you notes.

Lingerie Shower

This is the perfect shower for the bride who has everything. Typically, lingerie—or "personal" showers, as they're also known—are relatively small and intimate. After all, the bride may not feel comfortable opening and admiring lacy thongs and peek-a-boo teddies in front of her fiancé's grandmother. So if you're going to throw a lingerie shower, keep it small and intimate. Invite guests the bride feels comfortable with, such as her close girlfriends only. In addition to the aforementioned, gifts might include nighties, underwear, potpourri, lotions, perfumes, silk sheets, sexy books, and so on.

FACT

A lingerie shower is great because lingerie is not something many women are willing to splurge on themselves. Set the bride up with a good few years' worth of outfits!

This is meant to be a very girly shower. As such, you may wish to keep it in theme. Serve champagne, strawberries, and truffles. Give out small lotions or perfumes as shower gifts. Play games you wouldn't in mixed company. For example (if you think the bride will feel comfortable with it), invite everyone to tell their most risqué memory of the bride. Or have everyone write down their "wildest" experience, put it in a bowl, and have the bride read them one by one—guessing the author of each story. Create a serene, Victoria's Secret–type atmosphere with light classical music, aromatherapy candles, and low light.

Of course, don't throw a lingerie shower or include any activities that you suspect will make the bride uncomfortable. This is not the time to attempt to expand her horizons, even if *you* think it would be fun.

Holiday Shower

This is another great idea for the bride and groom who may already have many of the traditional shower gifts like linens and cookware. In this shower invitation, you'll assign each guest a specific holiday. Holidays might include Christmas, Halloween, Fourth of July, Flag Day, Rosh Hashanah, Easter, Chanukah, Kwanzaa–choose whatever holidays the bride and groom celebrate.

Guests are instructed to bring a gift that relates to those holidays. For instance, a guest assigned the Fourth of July may give the bride and groom a set of grill tools, or outdoor plates and bowls; for Christmas, gifts might include tree ornaments, decorations, a tree skirt, or a nativity set. This type of shower is a great way to help the bride and groom begin building a collection of holiday décor.

To tie the theme into the shower celebration, get creative. Have a "Christmas in July" shower at which you serve Christmas cookies, decorate with a small Christmas tree, and sing Christmas carols. Invite Santa to make an appearance (disguise the groom or the bride's father) to present gifts to the bride or to give small gift-wrapped favors to each guest.

ESSENTIAL

Before reserving a room or sending out invitations, be sure to check the shower date with the bride and her family. With so much going on, you don't want to risk scheduling the shower for the same day as another event.

Or conversely, have a Fourth of July in December party. Rent out a large indoor site where you can play indoor volleyball or tennis, or rent a hotel's indoor pool room or spa room for a few hours, where you can lounge, swim, and have a bite to eat. Serve barbecue, and drink summer cocktails.

Wine Shower

A wine shower is another great idea for the bride and groom who are already established with the household items they need. It's also a great theme shower to hold if the bride is being given multiple showers, and you want to host an event that's a little different from the others.

For a wine shower, you guessed it–guests give wine as gifts to the bride. If the bride and groom are wine enthusiasts, this is a wonderful way to jump-start a wine collection for their new home–or to supplement one they already have. Guests might bring local wines, specialty wines, bottles they've been saving—anything goes. They may also choose to bring wine-related gifts, such as wine corks, wine openers, wine chillers, or wine glasses.

Of course, a wine shower wouldn't be much fun without a wine tasting. When you plan this shower, you may decide to host your own tasting at home, or, if you're in proximity to a winery, you may want to hold the shower there. Often, wineries offer complimentary or low-cost tasting events, so be sure to call and negotiate on behalf of your group ahead of time. Remember, the winery benefits through exposure to a new audience, as well as through sales to those who visit.

For munchies, bring items such as crackers, cheeses, and finger foods to enjoy along with the wine, and see if the winery can accommodate the group afterward for a light lunch—bring it yourself or have it catered. Give each guest a pretty wine cork as a party favor.

Activity Shower

The activity shower is a great idea for the bride who'll have multiple showers, and for a party that will consist of ten or fewer guests. This shower revolves around an activity, such as ceramics, jewelry-making, or cooking lessons.

The venue can be a specialty shop where you can go with a small group and actually make things on-site, using their materials. For example, at a ceramics shop, you can hand-paint plates, bowls, mugs, and other specialty items. To incorporate this activity into a shower, choose one style of bowl or plate for all the guests to work on, choose a color scheme, and then have everyone paint and design the piece with her own creative flair.

At the end of the shower, the bride is given all the bowls or plates as a set for a shower gift—a very personal offering with great memories attached to it. (This would also be a fun warm-up to a bachelorette party.)

Couples Shower

The couples, or "coed," shower has grown increasingly popular in recent years. Clearly, as gender roles blur, so does the delineation between men and women when it comes to celebrating their very union. To some, the idea of holding events that separate males from females seems in direct conflict with the idea of marriage and the partnership between husband and wife. Whether you have strong beliefs about the issue or you just think it would be fun, a couples shower is an all-inclusive alternative to celebrate the bride and groom's impending nuptials.

For a couples shower, you'll obviously wish to cater to both the men and the women of the group. For that reason, these gatherings usually resemble engagement parties more than ladies' showers. They can still include many of the traditional shower activities, but the attendance of men certainly rules out, say, serving cucumber finger sandwiches and water with lemon as the featured menu items.

Plan this shindig as you would any other mixed gathering, with the addition of gift-giving as a featured activity. Yes, the bride should still engage in the traditional gift-opening session, except this time she's also joined by the groom. While enjoyable for the women, you may wish to incorporate an activity that will simultaneously amuse the men during the gift-opening session, like eating. And before or after the gifts, you may also wish to include shower games tailored to both sexes, like this version of the *Newlywed Game*.

A couples shower is more like an engagement party, except that the couple is expected to open their gifts while they're at the event, as with a traditional shower. It's the perfect alternative for the bride who has good friends who are both male and female.

Have two or three couples volunteer in advance to take part in competing against the bride and groom. Direct an impartial bridesmaid to ask each half of the couple the same questions in private immediately before the competition, so there's no cheating. The object is for the woman's answers to match the man's. Tailor the questions for your group—if it's an uptight group, for instance, try not to ask too many questions with the word "whoopee" in them. Questions might include these:

What's your least favorite chore? What's your spouse's biggest pet peeve? What quality do you like most about your spouse? What's your anniversary, including the date and year? Be creative with your questions.

Put the answers to the questions on big sheets of paper, so that they can be compared against each other with the shower guests as the "studio audience." The couple with the most matching answers–and the most points–wins a prize, which can be a gag gift or something of actual value.

You may also wish to set up the bride and groom to win beforehand, by giving them the answer to a difficult "bonus question." You'll get a lot of laughs when they actually get it right. Ask something they couldn't possibly know about each other, like the name of their first grade teacher, or their exact SAT scores.

Recipe Shower

If the bride does not want to receive shower gifts–but the bridesmaids still want to honor her with a get-together–a recipe shower is a great option.

You can do this a couple of ways. For either alternative, specify "no gifts" on the invitations. Your first option is to ask each guest to send you or another bridesmaid her favorite recipe prior to the shower date (a couple weeks in advance is recommended). You then use the recipes to create a personalized cookbook that will serve as a gift for the bride at the shower. Choose the craftiest or most computer-savvy bridesmaid to format and/or design the cookbook.

The second alternative is to send each guest a special card or page on which to write the recipe. Then bind all the pages together for a beautiful keepsake with a personal touch—each individual's handwriting. Create a cover and pretty binding for a gift the bride will cherish for years to come.

You're Invited!

So what should the shower invitation look like? Unlike the wedding invitation, shower invitations do not have to be extremely formal. There are plenty of predesigned, preprinted options available at wedding stationery stores, card stores, and other specialty stores if you want to fill in the information on each invitation by hand.

Or, to save time and energy, you may also decide to purchase preprinted invitations with all the vital information. These can be customized and ordered at a wedding stationery store.

A third and even less expensive option is to print the invitations yourself. With the evolution of personal color printer quality, the printing is much better and appropriate for invitations. Plus, you can purchase invitation "shells" with pretty designs at office supply stores and wedding stationery stores, and lay out the text to fit the graphics, for a professional look at a do-it-yourself price.

So what information should be included in the shower invitation? The following should cover the vitals:

- Name of the bride
- Type of party (bridal shower, couples shower, etc.)
- Date and time
- Address
- Name of hostess(es)
- RSVP date
- Phone number and e-mail address (if desired)
- Theme information, if applicable
- Shower registry information (optional)

There are two schools of thought regarding the inclusion of shower registry information in the invitation. (It's sometimes included in the invitation in the form of a separate business card, given by the registry store, or can be noted by the host at the bottom of the invitation.) The first school believes that this is a perfectly acceptable–and indeed practical–way of disseminating important information. The second school believes it's distasteful, and that it implies the guest's gift is more important than the guest's company.

FACT

In order to give guests—especially those from out of town—plenty of time to make arrangements to come to the shower, you should send out invitations four to six weeks in advance.

This is a matter of your personal taste. Obviously, there's no confusion about the objective of a shower—it's meant to set up the bride with the things she needs for her new home. Presumably, therefore, no one should really care if registry information is included—in fact, it might even make their lives a bit easier. But there will definitely be detractors who think including this information is inappropriate. If you're uncertain, solicit the bride's opinion. If she's uncomfortable with including the information, then don't do it.

Now that the shower's planned, what's next? The next big party is the one you've been waiting for—the bachelorette party!

Chapter 6

Unforgettable Bachelorette Parties

Planning the bachelorette party can be the most enjoyable aspect of being a bridesmaid. That's because there aren't a lot of rules. The bachelorette party is all about showing the bride a good time. And though as a sister event it has its roots in the traditional bachelor party—in other words, raucous and randy—bachelorette parties have also, in recent years, evolved in different directions to reflect more accurately the bride's sensibilities.

What Makes a Great Bachelorette Party?

While some brides still like the idea of a wild and crazy night on the town, other brides see the bachelorette party as an opportunity to relax and spend quality time with her closest friends and family members before she ties the knot.

No matter what, all bachelorette parties have one thing in common—they're events that bring the bride's girlfriends and/or close female relatives together for a day or evening (or weekend) of fun and companionship before the wedding. And planning and hosting them has become another of the bridesmaids' responsibilities as these parties have grown in popularity. In certain respects, the bachelorette party is probably a bit easier to plan than the shower, if only because there are few preset conventions to follow. The only difficulty will be narrowing down your many options.

FACT

Everyone's got a different definition of fun. While some brides-to-be may enjoy drinking and dancing 'til six in the morning, others may prefer a relaxing day at the spa with their closest friends. Be sure to plan something that suits the bride's temperament.

What's Your Bachelorette Style?

Because bachelorette parties began as a direct response to the bachelor party revelry that men have long enjoyed, it's only natural that they originally embraced the same basic tenets—bar- and club-hopping, strippers, and drinking to excess.

And while some brides thrive on the equality that the bachelorette party brings—and thoroughly enjoy these activities, to boot—other brides like the concept of togetherness but would prefer something a bit mellower (and just as much fun). There are additional factors, too, that will contribute to the style event you throw, most dominant among them being the guest list. While one style of party is perfectly appropriate for your ten sorority sisters, the same party may make, say, the mother and aunt of the bride extremely uncomfortable.

Very likely you can guess what tone event your bride would like—or perhaps she's let her wishes be known. If not, the following quiz is meant to help you determine what style party your bride would prefer.

1. When the bride's fiancé heads out for a night with the boys, what does the bride usually do?

a. Breathe a sigh of relief, get a pint of Ben & Jerry's, and settle down for a relaxing night with a new paperback.
b. Call a friend to enjoy a nice dinner out and a movie.
c. Get together with a group of girlfriends for a night of bar- and club-hopping 'till 3 A.M.

2. You're renting a movie with the bride. Which choice best symbolizes her preference?

   a. *Harry Potter* or the latest Disney flick
   b. *Being John Malkovich* or *Gosford Park*
   c. *Basic Instinct* or *Unfaithful*

3. Which best represents the bride's last vacation?

   a. A trip to Hilton Head with her parents and little brothers
   b. A weekend at Canyon Ranch with her sister
   c. A trip to Hedonism with her girlfriends

4. When the bride talks about a "wild time," what is she referring to?

   a. A few glasses of wine during Happy Hour with her sister
   b. Drinking, dancing, and flirting at a hot new club
   c. Skinny-dipping in a hot tub with two hot guys she just met

5. What best represents the bride's fashion sense?

   a. Ann Taylor
   b. Bebe
   c. Frankie B

If your answers were mostly "a": This girl tends to be more wholesome and conservative. Not much for the bar scene, this girl is probably more comfortable with a quiet evening of baby-sitting than with a wild night on the town.

Tread carefully when incorporating the racier aspects of the bachelorette party—even though it's a special evening, things like sexual props, daring games, and strippers may make her very uncomfortable. On the other hand, she may be waiting for a night like this to come out of her shell, so don't automatically assume that she wants kid stuff for her bachelorette, either.

Your best bet? Feel her out and see what her bachelorette tolerance level is.

If your answers were mostly "b": More of a sophisticate, this girl has been known to get jiggy with it–in a cool, classy way. While she may not enjoy wearing a "buck a bite" candy necklace for slobbering guys to pounce on, she will probably enjoy a night of good eats and upscale bar-hopping. Reservations at your city's hardest-to-get-into restaurant, followed by martinis at the hottest club, will do this bride-to-be just fine.

If your answers were mostly "c": For this bride, who puts the phrase "been there, done that" to shame, you'll really need to get creative.

This bride is sure to be satisfied with an out-of-towner where she can let it all hang out before the big day–a happening venue like New Orleans, Las Vegas, or New York might do the trick. Then again, you may be surprised–she may be through sowing her wild oats and prefer a quieter gathering of her closest girlfriends.

Definitely check with this wild child to determine her ultimate wishes.

The Guest List

Before you plan a minute of the bachelorette party, you'll probably want to pin down your guest list first. After all, you don't want to hire the stripper, rent the limo, and stock the bar only to discover that the bride's future mother-in-law will be in attendance. Then again, the bride's future mother-in-law may be young at heart and ready for a wild night of her own, so everything ultimately depends on the personalities of those involved.

So then who should be invited, anyway?

The Magic Number

The guest list should definitely be determined with the help of the bride. In general, bachelorette parties can range from a small group of five women to a much larger group of twenty to thirty, depending on your bride's particular circumstances. If she has a wide social circle and relatively open-minded relatives (and relatives-to-be), the bride may wish to include everyone.

On the other hand, the bride may prefer this event to be a smaller, more intimate gathering of her closest girlfriends and sisters, especially if she's expecting a night that's going to be on the bawdy side. Your best bet when noodling out the guest list is to assume nothing and to talk to the bride about her expectations. She may also appreciate your input and advice, based upon the type of event the bridesmaids are considering throwing.

This was the case with one Alexandria, Virginia, bride, who at twenty-eight had kept in touch with lots of friends from different areas of her life, including high school, college, and various jobs, not to mention her future sisters-in-law and women friends of her fiancé. If she included everyone, the guest list would have soared to at least twenty-five women.

FACT

Like the bridal shower, the bachelorette party planning and hosting duties should be delegated among the bridesmaids. So, too, should the cost—have each bridesmaid save her receipts, then add up everyone's costs and split them among the bridesmaids after the party.

But all that this busy bride envisioned was a simple sleepover at a friend's apartment, complete with wine, Chinese take-out, and some rented romance flicks. So she asked her bridesmaids to narrow down the list to five or six of her closest girlfriends, and to keep the evening small and simple. In fact, they chose not to call it a bachelorette party at all, just so no one would feel excluded.

On the other hand, a thirty-year-old bride from Indianapolis wanted something completely different. She had always dreamed of having a giant bash before her wedding, with all her women friends in attendance—her philosophy had always been the more, the merrier. So her bridesmaids planned a house party to accommodate a larger number (thirty-seven was the final count), complete with snacks, cocktails, and the requisite male stripper, and everyone had a great time.

Invitation Checklist

No matter how large or small the party will be, the following checklist will help ensure you don't forget to consider any important guests:

- All bridesmaids
- Bride's sisters
- Bride's cousins
- Bride's mother
- Bride's aunts
- Bride's future sisters-in-law
- Bride's future mother-in-law
- Any other of the bride's future in-laws
- Bride's childhood friends
- Bride's high school friends
- Bride's college friends
- Bride's coworkers
- Wives/girlfriends of groom's close friends

Once the guest list is established, be sure to send out invitations—or make phone calls—at least six weeks before the party date to ensure guests, especially those from out of town, have time to make the proper arrangements. Unlike showers, bachelorette party invitations are a bit more lax, with plans and invitations often traveling by word-of-mouth or e-mail. The more formal the event, the more formal your invitation should be.

Out on the Town

Now that you've narrowed down your bride's style, you've got a decent idea of the tone this party will take—and you've decided you'll definitely be heading out on the town. But there are still lots of options that range from racy to respectable—and who says the bachelorette party can't be both? The following are some ideas for specific theme parties that will take you outside the comforts of home. Take these ideas and follow them exactly, or give them your own unique spin to make them completely original.

Big Night Out

This event is perfect for the bride-to-be who doesn't get out with the girls very often and for the bride who can't get enough fun with her friends. The Big Night Out can be planned with many variations, but here's one that's universally fun.

Meet at one central place, like a bridesmaid's home or apartment. Have a few cocktails and munchies, play a warm-up bachelorette party game or two (see next section for ideas). Embark in your limousine, which you've hired in advance to escort your group anywhere it wants to go. (Develop a flexible itinerary ahead of time, so you'll have some consensus and/or ideas of where you want to go before the limo driver starts asking for destinations.) Pick at least one destination that's a bit of a drive, just so you can actually spend some time enjoying the limo before you start bar- and/or club-hopping.

Be sure to have some snacks on hand in the limo, to absorb what will presumably be a great deal of alcohol. Take advantage of games for the "outside world," also detailed later in this chapter. If you're feeling daring, escort the bride to a strip club for her last live glimpse at a naked stranger.

FACT

Props and games always make the big night out more fun (and will identify you immediately as a roaming bachelorette party). See Chapter 7 for ideas for bachelorette party activities, games, and novelties.

If you split the cost of the limo, the munchies, and the bar or club cover charges among all the bridesmaids—or even better, among all the attendees—this bachelorette party shouldn't cost a great deal of money. Expect to collect $50 to $75 per person, depending upon how many girls attend.

Obviously, the more attendees, the cheaper the night, but don't overstuff your limo, or you'll all be very uncomfortable. If you all go out to dinner, too, add an extra $25–$35 per person—unless you go somewhere really upscale, which will obviously end up costing a bit more.

A Sophisticated Dinner

What woman doesn't love the opportunity to try a great new restaurant? And there's no better excuse to splurge than a friend's or family member's bachelorette party. For this party, pick a restaurant that has very good food and an even better atmosphere—that is, don't pick a place that's too formal or stuffy, or you might risk attracting the ire of the entire restaurant as the girls start to let loose.

To avoid this unwelcome complication, choose a lively, happening restaurant with lots of young people and an understanding wait staff, and you'll be all set. Keep the wine and cocktails flowing, and hope for a waiter who'll willingly accept a little friendly abuse throughout the meal (like surprising him with penis straws in your water glasses, ordering a meal for the blowup doll, and so on). If you wish, have a limo (or a designated driver) take the group to a bar or club afterward to dance off that delicious and decadent dinner.

FACT

If you're going out to dinner, try to get reservations in your city's hottest, most happening restaurant. Call well in advance so you're sure to secure a spot.

The individual price per person at a group dinner always seems higher than at a dinner for two, probably because there are no holds barred when it comes to ordering appetizers for the table, keeping the drinks flowing, and ordering plenty of desserts and extras to share. This said, prepare to drop a little money on this evening, particularly if you'll be heading out afterward for more drinks and dancing or if you've hired a limo. The nice dinner out—when you've all split and added in the bride's expenses, too—will probably cost you at least a hundred bucks.

Comedy Club

A variation of the Big Night Out, this party idea makes the comedy club the focal event of the evening. If your group loves to laugh and you know there are some quality clubs in town, this may be an ideal pick for you. Of course, it may also be another limo stop on the "Big Night Out" circuit as well.

Keep in mind that many comedy clubs have cover charges and/or two-drink minimums, so call ahead to see if they'll offer your group a break or a special group rate. And be sure to let the comedians on stage know why you're there—very likely, the bride will become the center of some good-natured ribbing.

Every comedy club works differently. Call ahead, or check out your local clubs' Web sites to get the scoop on costs. Be sure to call in advance to negotiate group rates and also to reserve enough seats to accommodate your group.

There's No Place Like Home

While painting the town is always fun, sometimes there's nothing like the comfort of home. Throwing a home-based party can be an especially good option if there are a lot of guests coming in from out-of-town; without all the distractions of being out, you'll have more time to actually spend together—either catching up, or getting to know one another. And there are countless variations on the home party, if you get creative. So read on to discover if the home fires will be keeping you warm this bachelorette party season.

House Party

Like any house party you'd throw, this event can take on countless variations. The bare bones of this shindig, however, involve food, drinks, and some sort of entertainment. But aside from that, this house party can range from relaxed to raving.

Typically, this party would be hosted by one of the bridesmaids, with help from the others. You'll definitely want to prepare some food, which can range from a full dinner for a small crowd (if you're especially talented in the kitchen) to easy appetizers and munchies for a larger crowd. Or, to make it even simpler, order pizza or take-out for which everyone can chip in.

Depending on how ambitious (and understanding) you are, the house party can range from a small group (five to eight guests) to a much larger one (twenty guests or more). In fact, the house party is probably the best way to go if there's a large group of invited guests, only because coordinating a night of limos, dinner out, and bar-hopping can become a logistical nightmare for groups of more than ten. But that doesn't mean you'll have any less fun—bring the entertainment in-house, with games, props, and even a male stripper or two to keep guests lively and having fun.

FACT

When planning the bachelorette party, put one bridesmaid in charge of each task. Tasks might include food, alcohol, games, decorations/props, transportation, and other "entertainment" (wink, wink).

Of course, you can also give your party a theme to infuse some more character. A South-of-the-Border theme, for instance, would allow you to serve Mexican goodies like quesadillas, nachos, bean dips, and guacamole. It's also always fun to make blender drinks like frozen margaritas, especially with the girls when everyone's pitching in. Don't forget the penis piñata!

Another concept might include a wine-tasting theme, an idea to give the standard house party a more upscale edge (at least until everyone's buzz kicks in). Get a number of bottles of wines to test—both red and white—and run what amounts to a regular wine tasting. A good estimate is at least one bottle per person. Have plenty of water and plain crackers on hand to clean the palate in between tastings, and serve wine-friendly foods like fresh shellfish, a variety of cheeses, fruits, and crudités for guests to nibble on. Give each guest paper and pencil to write down their thoughts about each wine, and then compare them at the end. Give the bride a few bottles of wine as a special bachelorette party gift and remembrance.

Another in-house idea might include a "decadence" theme. The decadence theme is simply an excuse to indulge all the senses, girl-style. For this party you'd serve champagne and wine, a variety of good chocolates, and a full variety of sweet treats like chocolate-covered strawberries, éclairs, petits fours, cheesecakes—all the forbidden, decadent treats that are hard to resist. You might highlight this party by giving "forbidden" gifts to the bride as well, such as lingerie, erotic books, sex toys, or other bawdy gifts you couldn't bring yourself to present at the shower. Top the night off with a romantic or racy chick flick you can enjoy as you all digest your delicious, rich snacks.

QUESTION?

Do I have to give the bride a gift at her bachelorette party?

No, you do not have to give the bride another gift. However, you may wish to give the bride a gag gift or two of bachelorette-related items—these are hard to resist. Go online to find countless fun and goofy bachelorette gifts.

The cost of the house party can range depending on the food and alcohol you serve, and how elaborate you choose to get with favors, gifts, and decorations. However, with everyone pitching in, this is probably the least expensive route to go, even if you decide to serve lobster tails to fifteen guests. Of course, if you order a stripper (another decadent option) it will up the ante by $150 or more, but split among say, ten people, it's only an extra $15 to $25. And won't the look on the bride's face as this studly man gives her his undivided attention be completely priceless, anyway?

The Throwback Slumber Party

Unlike other house parties that may end around midnight, that's the time the slumber party just gets going! Like slumber parties of yore, the primary activities of this party are to stay up all night, giggle, make prank phone calls, and confess all your pent-up secrets. You may wish to keep this party relatively small to better accommodate a stroll down memory lane.

For example, if you invite the bride's closest friends from high school, be sure to bring out the old photos and yearbooks, and relive those seemingly long-lost glory days. Ask all the guests/bridesmaids to raid their closets for anything they might have saved from those days—old notes, love letters, teen magazines, anything they're willing to share with the group.

For eats, have plenty of foods on hand that you regularly scarfed down during your teenage years—tortilla chips, cheese dip, microwave pizza bagels and mozzarella sticks, popcorn, and soda. Of course, now that you're that you're of age, you can actually add alcohol to this gathering legally—and you won't have to spend half the night strategizing how and where you're going to get it.

This party is about as low cost as you can get. Your biggest expense might be a sheet pizza or a case of hooch. (Or those long-distance charges you've racked up pranking all your ex-boyfriends.) But you'll definitely get a lot of bang for your buck, and you'll be able to spend some genuine quality time together.

ESSENTIAL

A house party can be a cost-effective alternative to a night on the town. Plus, you can get as creative as you like with the theme, food, decorations, games, or other forms of entertainment.

Poker Night

Again, why should the boys have all the fun? Poker night is a perfect way for the girls to get together, bond, and win a little cash.

To properly host poker night, be sure to have a number of round tables that seat four to five people; plenty of decks of cards (get some naked-man playing cards to stay in theme); poker chips that guests can "purchase" when they arrive; available cigars and cigarettes to create the requisite smoky atmosphere; and plenty of good beer and single-malt scotch to smooth out the rough edges.

Don't forget some music in the background and some tasty munchies for what's sure to be a long, fun evening. You may also wish to run a fifty/fifty split raffle.

To do this, sell tickets for a couple bucks apiece (double-sided tickets that are sold on long rolls are perfect). At the end of the night, pick a ticket—the winner gets half the proceeds of the ticket sales, and the bride gets the other half.

QUESTION?

We'd love to do poker night, but not everyone plays. What should we do?
If not everyone is a poker shark (a likely scenario), hire a poker instructor to give a quick lesson at the beginning of the party. Then make poker night an excuse for a semiregular girls' night out.

Poker night is a comparatively cheap evening, especially if you don't have a losing streak. Of course, you can organize poker night with fake money, allocating a certain number of chips per guest as they come in, or you can gamble with real money, charging, say, a dollar per chip. The only other expense will be munchies, drinks, and those naked-man playing cards, which you wouldn't dream of doing without.

Coed Party

Though "coed bachelorette party" may seem a paradox, it's possible to combine the sexes for a night of fun and prenuptial mayhem. There are certain cases when this might make sense for your group.

Perhaps you have a social group that's very mixed, and the bride would miss having her close male friends around; or perhaps the bride and groom have decided they'd rather combine their bachelor and bachelorette parties into one big fun event. Maybe the bride and groom are fundamentally opposed to separating groups based solely on gender. Whatever the reason, it's easy to include everyone in parties like Big Night Out, a sports-related party, or a house party. Even a throwback slumber party would have a whole new dimension with the addition of boys . . . bring your cutest PJs!

Plan this party as you would any other party—perhaps it's a theme party (James Bond masquerade party, Mexican fiesta theme), a simple house party, or perhaps it's renting a room at a local restaurant or bar. Feel free to use any of the bachelorette party ideas in this chapter—just add boys!

Some would say the highest cost would be the loss of a girls-only get-together. But if the bride doesn't want to exclude anyone, or if she'd prefer joining forces—hey, the more, the merrier.

The Weekend Getaway

The weekend getaway doubles as a mini-vacation for all the guests. It can be a great way to spend relaxed time together without constant distractions.

The weekend (or long weekend) getaway might take you anywhere. Good bachelorette party destinations might be a condo in a ski town; an all-inclusive tropical resort, such as Club Med; a stylish new hotel and casino (they're popping up all over); or a weekend of pampering at a spa.

No matter what destination you ultimately choose, take some time beforehand to organize a flexible itinerary, so that the weekend will have some structure. For example, if you're staying at a ski resort condo, perhaps Saturday and Sunday morning and afternoon will be reserved for ski time, while Friday night you'll head out on the town and Saturday evening you'll put together a homemade feast and play board games at the condo.

No matter where you go, weekend getaways offer the time and means to relax and spend quality bonding time together before the big day.

ALERT!

If you know most of the bridesmaids and potential guests are strapped for cash, don't push the idea of a weekend getaway for a bachelorette party. There are plenty of fun things you can still do close to home.

A weekend getaway is probably the costliest alternative for a bachelorette party, due to travel costs, accommodations, and incidental costs. Of course, there are always methods to cut those costs, like going to a destination that's within driving distance, sharing the cost of a condo or rental unit among the group, and bringing food and drinks with you. Obviously, a trip to Club Med will cost more than a weekend camping trip, so if you think that many of those on your invite list can't swing it, you may wish to plan something within easier financial reach. Most likely the bride would prefer to include as many of her close friends as possible and stick closer to home than to plan some elaborate getaway that only two of her friends can attend.

The Sports-Related Event

Why should those fun, all-day golf outings be reserved for just the bachelors? Even if all the girls aren't great golfers, getting out on the course for a day of duffing—or some other fitness-related event—will afford you the outdoors, sun, snacks, and togetherness that the boys have long enjoyed.

Your options certainly aren't limited to golf—perhaps you'd rather organize an informal tennis tournament followed by a beach barbecue, or a bike trip to a scenic destination where you can all enjoy a picnic. No matter what the bride's favorite sport or activity, you can definitely turn it into an excuse for an outdoors bachelorette party that's a unique and healthful alternative to the drinking and bar-hopping event. It's always possible, too, that your sporting ways may just be a precursor to less health-minded evening activities—why should the fun stop if your group doesn't want it to?

If it's a golf outing, fees can range from $30 to $50 or more per person, depending on the course. If you plan a tennis tournament, hike, or bike trip, the only cost you'll likely have will be for food and drinks. So comparatively, this type of outing will be healthful for your heart–and your wallet.

FACT

If you're planning a golf outing for a group that includes nongolfers, choose a shorter, "executive" style course or a par-three course. These courses generally host less experienced golfers who won't get too frustrated as you go for your tenth shot on a par-three hole.

Chapter 7

It's All Fun and Games

Games and activities have always been a part of the bridal shower tradition. And now the tradition has extended (usually with a bit more edge) to the bachelorette party, as well. You can make them as unique and creative as you want to, or as raunchy as you want. They are all about having a good time. This chapter contains guidelines and ideas for incorporating activities into your event, ranging from the subdued to the sophisticated to the downright spicy.

Shower Game Basics

Part of the grand history of showers is a little game-playing among the ladies. Games can often serve as ice-breakers, fostering interaction among guests who don't know each other, or they can just serve as a fun diversion between eating and gift-opening. (Or during gift-opening, which can seem interminable—especially at large showers.)

Shower games can range from corny to goofy to somewhat sophisticated. Women seem to fall on either end of the spectrum when it comes to their feelings about shower games. Some women can't tolerate them and dread the moment they begin. Other women, though, wouldn't consider it a proper shower without them.

What Kind and How Many?

Choose your games carefully, and tailor them to the group at hand. Don't choose a game that requires guests to bare their souls if you know you have a conservative group. Choose age- and personality-appropriate games, and everyone is sure to be enthusiastic.

ESSENTIAL

Choose games that are appropriate for your group's general demographics—young, older, mixed, coed. For instance, not many men would enjoy the spice game, where guests guess which spice is which.

Two to four games during a shower are usually appropriate—any more, and your guests may start to lose interest. Remember to have plenty of pens and paper on hand, as well as firm surfaces on which to write if guests aren't seated at tables (magazines usually do the trick). And don't forget the prizes!

Prizes

Prizes are a great way to get guests more involved and enthusiastic about playing shower games. But how much should you spend on prizes, and what items are appropriate?

Your best bet is to offer small gifts that will have universal appeal. Ideas include candles, potpourri, body lotions, small perfumes, candy or chocolate, gourmet food items, pretty kitchen towels, small flower arrangements, trinket boxes, paperweights, bookmarks, pens, novelty kitchen timers, bath soaps, small photo albums, sachets—the list is endless. You may also wish to include one grand prize, such as a bottle of wine or champagne, a basket of lotions and shampoos, or another item you think your guests might like.

Game Ideas

There are countless games you can play at showers. Some of the following may be familiar to you from showers you've attended in the past, or they may be games you've never heard of. Remember—choose the games you feel your particular group will be enthusiastic about playing, and have one bridesmaid in charge running them smoothly.

The Name Game

This is a simple, quiet game guests can play throughout the shower. At the top of a piece of paper, write the bride's and groom's names–for instance, Kimberly and Scott. The guest who creates the most new words using the letters of the names wins. For example, words derived from these two names would include "kilt," "bet," "best," or "toy."

Wedding Song

As each guest enters, supply her with a small sheet of paper to jot down her wedding song (or her favorite song with a boyfriend, if she's not married). Later in the party, have the bride announce each of the songs that have been written down; guests then guess whom each song belongs to.

The person with the most correct guesses wins–bonus points if she guesses what song the bride and groom have chosen. This is a fun way of discovering the wedding songs of family and friends, especially of older guests.

Bridal Bingo

This game takes a little advance prep work, but it's a fun diversion during the gift-opening session. To play bridal bingo, give each guest a customized bingo card (for fun, write the letters B-R-I-D-E at the top, or

M-A-R-R-Y). In each square, write the name of a popular shower gift. These might include blender, plate, pitcher, cheese grater, toaster, lingerie, colander, frying pan, spatula, pillowcases, bath towels, and so on. (Have all the bridesmaids chip in to make these cards, as it can be a bit time-consuming.)

As the bride opens a gift that matches an item in the bingo square, the guest can cover it or cross it off. When she gets five in a row, she yells "Bingo!" and wins a prize. Much fanfare can be made of "checking her numbers" against the gifts already opened. And like regular bingo, you can continue playing the game until someone covers four corners, the inside square, or her whole card.

Spice Girls

This is a fun game for all ages, and would make a great tie-in to a kitchen theme shower. Take about ten spices and cover the labels with the letters *A* through *J*. Then pass them around, and ask guests to identify each spice. Have them write their answers on a sheet of paper, indicating each spice by its letter. At the end of the game, reveal the spices—the guest with the most correct matches wins.

Safety-Pin Game

This is a silly game that will keep guests on their toes. Give each guest a safety pin when they arrive to pin to their shirt or scarf. Then pick a word that you think will be used fairly often at the shower, such as "bride," "groom," or "wedding." Tell the guests that this word is off-limits over the course of the shower.

If a guest is caught using it, whoever caught her can take her safety pin away. Maybe she has already collected a safety pin or more from other loose-tongued guests; if so, she has to give up all the pins she's collected in addition to her own. Whoever collects the most safety pins by the end of the shower is the winner.

Purse Game

This hearkens back to the old game show *Let's Make a Deal.* At various intervals during the gift-opening session, one of the bridesmaids will act as emcee, announcing to guests that they'll be playing the purse game. The bridesmaid will then announce random items, and if a guest happens to have that item in her purse, she wins a prize.

The more obscure the item, the bigger and better the prize. It's a funny way to see what women will actually schlep around in their purses. Try items like "underwear," "sugar packets," "foreign currency," "condoms"—whatever you think would be fun and appropriate for your particular group.

Welcome Shower Diversions

Of course, there's no specific formula you need to stick to when hosting a shower. You can add or subtract anything to kick things up a notch. From practical to sentimental, added shower activities can really help reflect the true meaning behind the shower and the coming wedding. They can also help guests connect in a whole new way.

The following are a few ideas to get you thinking about additional activities for your shower.

Create-a-Scrapbook

Making a scrapbook for the bride involves a small investment in guests' time before the shower. Along with the shower invitation, send a blank page from a scrapbook or photo album. Invite each guest to design a page for the bride using pictures, poems, artwork–anything goes. It should simply reflect the guest's feelings or relationship with the bride. The guest should then bring the page to the shower to add it to an album, which will be presented to the bride as she's opening her gifts. (This is best done as a surprise.)

FACT

A special shower activity can be inspiring and help connect guests to one another. Choose something that allows guests to reflect on the meaning of marriage or that brings up personal memories of the bride.

Who wouldn't love a scrapbook album with mementos and thoughts from one's closest friends and family members? This is truly a gift the bride will keep and treasure forever, and guests will enjoy looking at all the pages of memories from fellow friends and family members.

Bridal Quiz Show

The bridal quiz show begins by giving guests a page with questions about the bride, to which the bride has supplied answers (to you only) prior to the shower. You can ask questions from all facets of the bride's life, such as the name of her first pet; the name of her first boyfriend; her major in college; her most embarrassing moment; her proudest moment; the thing she loves most about the groom.

When guests are finished completing questions, one bridesmaid can announce the answers. For added fun, give the quiz to the groom before the shower, and read his answers aloud, along with the bride's, to see how much he really knows about his beloved. Undoubtedly, his input will make for a good laugh or two.

The person with the most correct answers can be given a prize or memento.

FACT

The bridal quiz show is a great way to catch up with the bride while providing a little competition for the guests. It also provides a good forum to test the groom's knowledge—like a mini *Newlywed Game*!

What Makes a Good Marriage?

As guests arrive, give them a sheet of paper and a pen and ask them to share one tip about what they feel makes a good marriage. Then, as a break from opening gifts, have the bride read these tips aloud to the group.

For added fun, have the group guess who wrote each individual tip. Inevitably, you will get a full range of ideas, from silly to sentimental. But no matter what the advice, it's a game that really brings to light the meaning of the bridal shower–and reminds the remaining guests of what marriage is all about.

Bridal Clone

This is a quick, fun activity that can also double as a game. In advance of the shower, make a list of characteristics that start out quite general but get more specific as the game goes along. The object is to see who is most like the bride. You might start off by saying, "Like the bride, you have blue eyes." Everyone with blue eyes remains standing; everyone without them sits down and is out of the game.

Then go on to a question like, "Like the bride, you have a bachelor's degree," followed by "Like the bride, you play tennis." The end statements should get quite specific, such as "Like the bride, you're wearing red underwear right now." Be creative and make up fun questions that relate to your particular bride.

Then give a prize to the last woman standing, and announce that it is she who is closest to being the bridal clone.

Funniest Memory

If your group is big on laughs, this is a game that keeps them coming. As guests enter the party, give them a sheet of paper and pen to write down the funniest memory that they share with the bride.

Once everyone has written their memory, give them to the bride to look through and read aloud. The bride can then elaborate, relaying the funny story to the group. This activity works especially well if the bride can ham it up and tell a good story. It may fall flat and make her uncomfortable if she's shy in front of groups.

Creative Basket

This is a shower gift and an activity rolled into one. If there's a particularly creative bridesmaid, she may be able to take charge of this one. The creative basket is a great gift for bridesmaids to give, as a supplement to hosting the shower, especially if you've already given the bride gifts at other showers.

It goes like this. Buy a bunch of brand-name products from the supermarket, the names of which you can incorporate into a story about the bride and groom. For example, one sentence might go like this. "As the bride waited months and months for her groom to propose, she knew something would have to 'Tide' her over until she'd see that ring 'Sparkle' on her finger. So she made a 'Dash' for the border for a 'Bold' weekend of fun and excitement in Tijuana with her girlfriends . . . until it 'Dawn'ed on her that she was really much happier with her man."

Create a gift basket of all the products used in the story, then lift them out as you recite the story aloud for the group. It's a clever way to give the bride household items she'll inevitably need—and to tell a fun story that specifically relates to the bride and groom.

 **FACT**

Games are a great ice-breaker, especially among groups of women who may not already know each other. They're also an excuse for the bride to bring out her wild side with impunity.

Bachelorette Party Games

Like shower games, bachelorette party games provide a great forum for guests to interact (with each other and with the outside world). Whether you're staying in or going out, there are plenty of fun games you can play to commemorate the occasion with true style and lots of laughs.

Fun Games for Home

If you're staying in for the night, these games will provide some fun (and sometimes goofy) diversions.

Pin the "Tail" on the Man

A variation of the classic game, except this time the tail's in front. For even more fun and frivolity (and if the bride won't object) blow up a picture of the groom (clothed, of course) and use him as the target in question. Or, paste a picture of his face over the model's.

First Kiss

This is a fun girls-only game for relatively small groups of under ten. Each guest first tells her first-kiss story (presumably from her younger days), followed by her first-kiss story with her current man. The guests then vote on the best first-kiss story from each category. Have bachelorette-themed prizes on hand for the winners.

How Well Does the Bride Know the Groom?

Before the bachelorette party, have one of the bridesmaids go on a fact-finding mission to get info from the groom. Questions she asks may range from the innocent (What was your first dog's name? What is your worst pet peeve?) to the relatively risqué (What's your favorite body part? What's your wildest time with the bride?).

At the bachelorette party, the bride is asked to guess the groom's answers to each question. By the end of the quiz, it will become apparent how well the bride really knows her groom.

I Never

This game can be played with or without drinking. Guests sit together in a circle. Each guest goes in turn, with a declaration of something she's never done. For example, the first guest might say, "I've never kissed two guys in one night." Any guest who actually has done this must confess by taking a sip of her drink (or throwing in a poker chip, or a penny, or any alternate token).

The play then proceeds to the right, with the next guest giving a new "I never." This game tends to get racier as it goes on, and it's amazing to find what your friends will confess to, especially after a few drinks.

Games for the Outside World

If you're out on the town, these games will help your group make many new friends or—at the very least—provide the bride with a little extra attention.

Suck for a Buck

There are plenty of premade kits for this type of activity, but you can also fashion your own. This "game" involves giving the bride a special T-shirt with Lifesavers or other hard candies attached to it—either with safety pins, sewn on, or stuck on with a swipe of water (the more strategic the candy placement, the more titillating the game).

Then, when she is out and about, she (or her friends and bridesmaids) offers passersby the opportunity to take a "suck for a buck." This also works with a candy necklace, if the bride wishes to wear her own outfit. Definitely an ice-breaker with the bar crowd.

Very Daring

At the start of the night, present the bride with a list of dares that she must complete by the evening's end. These dares might include tasks that range from the relatively easy to the increasingly difficult.

For example, the first task might be telling the group about her first date with her fiancé; while the tenth dare might involve getting a pair of man's boxers by the night's end. Other dares might include standing on a chair in a public place and announcing "I'm getting married" five times; doing suggestive shots, like the famous "sex on the beach"; or getting the business cards of ten single guys.

Scavenger Hunt

This is a great game for bachelorette parties that are both in and out of the house. For the scavenger hunt, guests are broken up into teams. Each team is given a list of items they need to return to the party with, in a determined amount of time (an hour or two is best). Each item is assigned a point value, with difficult items being awarded a higher score. Items should definitely be bachelorette party related or related to your childhood/adolescence (sentimental value).

ALERT!

If you're planning a scavenger hunt, and the group will be driving to find the items on their lists, be sure to insist that everyone obeys traffic rules—no crazy driving to get around faster. Also, no drinking until after the hunt is over.

The following are some examples in each point category.

1 Point

A temporary tattoo (applied to one of the team members, of course)
A condom
An X-rated magazine
A fortune cookie
A copy of the bridal registry

5 points

A pair of handcuffs
A poker chip from a casino
A cigar
A deck of naked-man playing cards
An X-rated video
A bridal veil

10 points

An old rotary phone
A pair of the groom's underwear
An eight-track tape
A pair of leg warmers
An old Shaker-knit sweater from The Limited
A red lace garter belt

20 points

Seahorses
A Viagra pill

A vibrator
An original Merlin or Simon game

50 points
A male stripper

Paying Your Props

The bachelorette party would not be complete without the props geared toward the single gal's last hurrah. And there are plenty of them. In the last ten years, an entire bachelorette party industry has sprung up to meet every girl's need for penis straws, naked-man playing cards, and much, much more.

They're much easier to come by now, too. Although many of the items previously required a trip to the (sometimes) seedy "adult" store in town, today's bachelorette items are more readily available. Find them in novelty stores such as Spencer gifts, party supply stores, and easiest of all on the Internet, in online venues like *www.bacheloretteparties.com.*

And while they are ultimately sillier than they are salacious (kind of like male strippers), that's precisely why they're so much fun. Consider incorporating some of the following into your bachelorette bash:

- Penis piñatas
- Willy Whack-It Piñatas—a variation of the plain penis piñata
- Suck for a Buck T-shirt and Candy Kit—everything

you need to make the bride a T-shirt that offers passing barflies the opportunity to suck a candy—off her shirt—for a buck (put the proceeds toward blow-job shots)

- Glow-in-the-Dark Pecker Toss Game—a game of chance for home competition
- Gummy Butts and Gummy Penises—for the hungry crowd
- X-Rated Fortune Cookies—surprise your friends and family with what's inside
- Penis-shaped Jell-O shot tray—makes Jell-O shots even more exciting than usual!
- Pecker earrings—for the discriminating bachelorette fashionista
- Bling-Bling 100-carat ring—almost as big as J. Lo's!
- Belly jewelry and body glitter—for the subtler bachelorette
- Pecker lantern—lighting the way to the bathroom as you toss your bachelorette party cookies
- X-rated karaoke microphone—is it a penis or a microphone cover? Fool your friends!
- Glow-in-the-dark blowup dolls—perfect company for the bride, when her fiancé doesn't make it home from his own bachelor party
- Pink Nubby Cock Candles—look out, Martha Stewart, this is real style
- Pecker Party Lights—the perfect decorative complement to Pink Nubby Cock Candles
- Tantalizing toilet paper—just try not to get aroused by the naked stick figures pictured here!

So what should you do with all these props? Perhaps you'd like to make your dinner for seven a dinner for eight, with your blowup doll in tow; maybe the bride can show off her Bling Bling ring to inquiring parties at the bars. The gummy butts, gummy penises, and cock candles are the perfect accents to your house party. Get creative. Show off your props with pride.

ESSENTIAL

Bachelorette party–inspired props are a fun way to differentiate the occasion from any other night on the town. Time how long it takes the bartender to notice your penis earrings, or the waiter to spy those penis straws you've surreptitiously placed in your margaritas.

Now That's Entertainment!

There's one more important prop you may wish to include in your bachelorette party celebration—the stripper. Should every bachelorette party include one? And how do you find him?

Good Idea?

Again, the bride will probably have a pretty definite opinion about whether or not she'd welcome a male stripper. Obviously, you might want his arrival to be a surprise, so you may wish to do some sleuthing to determine if the bride would approve or not. Try this method: Tell her a story about a bachelorette party you recently attended that featured a stripper (make up the story if you need to).

If she's against the idea of strippers, she'll probably seize the opportunity to let you know. "How gross" or "That's tacky" are pretty certain signifiers that she's against it. However, if her reaction is "How fun," or "Was he hot?" it may indicate she's open to the idea. Obviously, besides the bride's wishes you'll also need to factor in the guest list when considering a stripper; if it's a large party with in-laws and older generations in attendance, a stripper may not be the best idea.

But if you *do* want to hire a stripper, what should you expect?

How Do I Find Him?

The thought of hiring a stripper may fill you with some trepidation. Will you have to go to some seedy strip club to point and pick? Or worse, will you call, give your credit card number, and then wait in vain for someone from the "agency" to show up, only to find later you've been charged double–for nothing?

Luckily, hiring your man is as easy as flipping through the Yellow Pages. While "strippers" will probably not yield the results you're looking for (too obvious for the phone book people, perhaps), "Entertainment" or "Entertainers" will. Most likely, there will be large display ads as well as the regular listings–hey, this is big business. You're bound to find at least a few appropriate listings right away.

Be sure to treat your stripper with respect. He is simply making a living, and while he may seem as if he's got unflappable confidence when he's standing before you like a modern-day Adonis, that's no reason to insult him or question his choice of occupation.

To avoid being put into any compromising position (no pun intended), be sure to ask the following questions when hiring your guy:

- What will this service cost? Is there one flat rate, or can you order extras à la carte?
- How long will the performance be? (That's minutes, not inches.)
- Will an encore cost more?
- What forms of payment are accepted, and when do you have to pay? (Some services will ask for half in advance, and the other half upon completion of services.)
- Can you see your guy in advance? Is there a video of him, or a place where you can take a sneak peak at his performing style?
- Can he wear something specific? Perhaps you want to goof on the bachelorette by ordering a dancer in doctor garb (her current fiancé's occupation), or in fireman's garb (like her last beau).
- What if he doesn't show up? Are you entitled to some sort of refund, and/or is there a backup to take his place?
- What, exactly, will he do? Take it all off, strip down to a G-string, what? You should probably be (at

least mentally) prepared if he's going to strip down completely.

ALERT!

Avoid Fabio wanna-bes by asking if the agency will allow you to choose your specific stripper by looking through photos. Perhaps they have such a service available online.

Of course, you can skip all the sleuthing by bringing the horse to water, so to speak, and visiting a strip club yourselves. If there's one in your town or a nearby destination, going to a strip club will be an event you won't soon forget. Full of whooping, laughing women, the male strip club resembles a comedy club more than a seedy or sexy strip club—aside, of course, from the unclad men.

If you plan to take your bachelorette party to the club instead of ordering "take-out," call the club ahead of time to see if there are any group rates or special rooms your party can take advantage of. Then the bride can pick her favorite from a wide variety of onstage hotties.

You're sure to have a blast creating a night that the bride will not soon forget.

Chapter 8

The Wedding Day

It's the moment we've all been waiting for. Or the twelve hours of moments we've been waiting for. All the buildup, all the planning, and all the celebration are finally culminating in this moment. And while you've most likely attended a wedding or two, you may never have been a behind-the-scenes player, where all the real, down-to-the-wire action is taking place—alongside the bride. Here's the lowdown on what you can expect on the big day.

Pregame Warm-Up

The wedding day action typically begins well before the scheduled events. In fact, between the preparation, ceremony, reception, and after-hours, a wedding adds up to being a very long day. That said, the most important way you can prepare for the day ahead will occur on the night before.

That's right—it all begins with a good night's sleep. It may be difficult to heed this advice, particularly if the rehearsal dinner is held the night before the wedding. You may find it disappointing to put a sudden end to the celebration with friends or family you haven't seen in a while, after all. But if you've got to get up at seven to begin your day, even a professional makeup artist and hair stylist will find it a challenge to work with the results of four hours' sleep. And feeling good? Forget about it. You'll be a walking zombie.

So what will the day entail and how can you, beautiful bridesmaid, best get through it? Read ahead to learn just what you can expect.

The Countdown Begins

Weddings are like the Academy Awards. One often spends more time getting ready for the event than actually *at* the event. And as maid of honor or bridesmaid, you are definitely along for the preparty ride. Even though you're playing supporting actress to the bride's superstar, you will nevertheless experience some of the glow from the spotlight, which means you'll want to look your best.

The Salon Experience

A nice tradition that many brides are practicing today is the scheduling of group beauty treatments for the bridesmaids on the morning of the wedding. Sometimes the bride will foot the bill for these treatments as a special wedding-day treat for the bridesmaids, but she may also expect you to pay for them yourself—and/or give you the choice to opt out.

If you're on the fence about whether or not to participate, keep in mind that this is a time-honored ritual whose pleasures may come as a surprise—a group of excited and gabby girlfriends, all of whom are being pampered by hired stylists. It's a great time to relax, laugh, and bond a little before the pressures of the day take over.

FACT

Go the extra mile for your bride by offering to schedule the bridal party's wedding-day beauty appointments. This can often be logistically complicated, particularly if bridesmaids are each having more than one service or treatment. It'll be a weight off the bride's mind!

The bride has probably cornered a number of stylists at her favorite salon to provide hair, makeup, manicures, or pedicures as a group. Ideally, one bridesmaid should be getting a pedicure while another's getting her makeup done while another's getting her hair done, so that you can all cycle around and take full advantage of the time you're at the salon.

If you'd like, offer to help the bride with this task in advance of the wedding day. Coordinate all the bridesmaids' appointments and have them written down in an accessible location on the day of the wedding, so there is no confusion. It's also best to confirm these appointments a week in advance to avoid any wedding-day mini-tragedies or misunderstandings.

If you're thinking of begging off from the beauty treatments on the morning of the wedding, remember that this is usually a nice time to relax and unwind before the wedding mayhem actually begins. And as much as you may cringe at paying for something you can do yourself, remember that you definitely want to look your best—a month from now as you look at the bride's photography proofs you may regret not having your hair or makeup professionally done. And don't underestimate the relief you'll experience by letting someone *else* worry about getting your hair and makeup perfect, for a change. Avoid the bad hair day.

Bridesmaids' Luncheon

If there is enough time on the wedding day, the bride may also host a bridesmaids' luncheon, also known as a bridesmaids' tea. This event may also be held in the days leading up to the wedding. While not all brides honor this tradition, it can be a nice, relaxing event that gathers the bridesmaids together one last time before the wedding actually occurs. It's often held at the bride's or her mother's home, and is meant to honor the bridesmaids and to show the bride's appreciation for all her maids have done.

The bride often uses this opportunity to present her bridesmaids with traditional small gifts as thanks. These gifts might consist of items ranging from jewelry or handbags to be worn with the bridesmaid dresses; picture frames or albums; small keepsakes such as elegant key rings or hand-sized mirrors; or practical yet pretty gifts such as personalized stationery. For the bridesmaids' luncheon, you have no duties except to attend, enjoy, and accept the bride's thanks graciously.

Free Time

Of course, not every bride will have professional services scheduled for the bridesmaids, or even for herself. And some brides may simply prefer solitude in the hours leading up to the wedding frenzy. Presumably, this will leave you with a lot of free time, especially if the wedding doesn't begin until early evening. What's a fidgety bridesmaid to do, especially if she's from out of town and stuck in a hotel room?

Salon Appointments

First, you can schedule your own beauty treatments independently, if you so desire. Use your friend's wedding as a great excuse to treat yourself to a little prenup pampering. If you're staying out of town, research whether your hotel offers spa or beauty services, or if you can take advantage of a nearby salon.

Even if you don't want your hair or makeup professionally styled, this might be the perfect time for a massage, facial, or even a simple manicure. Get together with a friend, another bridesmaid, or your date, and spoil yourselves for a few hours.

ALERT!

When it comes to travel and activity in the hours before the wedding, always err on the side of caution. Fly into town a day earlier than you need to. Don't schedule a major sightseeing tour on the morning of the wedding. And give yourself plenty of time to primp, in case of any girl-type disasters.

Sightseeing

Being an out-of-town visitor offers further opportunities to fill your time in the hours leading up to the wedding. Visit local landmarks, museums, and galleries. Take advantage of the shopping. Or have a long, leisurely lunch at a great restaurant.

Of course, if you're in from out of town, there are probably friends or family members to visit. Make plans with them in advance so you have your days organized before you arrive, and so you're sure they won't make separate plans of their own before you've had a chance to talk to them.

Socializing with the Boys

By the way, the groomsmen will be having this same dilemma. If they, like the bridesmaids, are looking for something to do, perhaps you might arrange a little social gathering during the hours leading up to the wedding. If you have access to a pool or beach, invite everyone over to kick back and relax for a few hours before they have to get ready. You can plan a golf outing, a hike, or a luncheon, or you might ask the hotel if they'll open up a hospitality suite for you all to hang out in before the wedding begins.

Watch the Clock

Beware, however, of overstuffing the wedding day with activities. One bridesmaid visiting Buffalo, New York, thought she'd have plenty of time to visit Niagara Falls—a thirty-minute drive—in the hours before the wedding. Unfortunately, she and her date got lost driving back, and she just barely made it to the church on time—to the consternation of an already stressed-out bride. The bottom line—plan something with a controlled time limit, and be sure to pad your primping time in case of any unforeseen circumstances.

De-Stressing the Bride

As a bridesmaid, one of your unwritten but integral duties throughout the engagement period is to provide moral support for the bride. At no time will this be more vital, probably, than on the wedding day itself.

Unless she's on some serious mood-altering drugs, the bride will inevitably be somewhat nervous in the hours leading up to the wedding ceremony. It's understandable–when you've spent literally hundreds of hours planning and poring over the details of a one-day event, you tend to invest a lot of yourself in that event's success. Add to that the emotional impact of committing yourself to lifelong marriage, and it's impossible not to feel the pressure.

FACT

A nervous bride is a natural part of weddings. Do what you can to provide moral support, troubleshooting, and laughter to relieve her wedding-day jitters.

Plus, there's the added stress of being on display in front of hundreds of your nearest and dearest, which becomes much more real as the wedding grows closer. And if, by chance, any unexpected circumstances should arise (a hurricane hits, a bridesmaid gets the stomach flu, the flowers never show up), we're talking real tension.

So what can you, dear bridesmaid, do to alleviate her stress? Try some of the following tactics to help calm the bride's somersaulting stomach in the hours leading up to the biggest commitment she'll ever make.

Make Her Laugh

There's no better tension relief than laughter. And you know best what the bride thinks is funny. Save a humorous anecdote to tell her the day of the wedding, download some of those goofy puns she loves, or relive funny old stories to keep her relaxed.

Suggest a Massage or Spa Treatment

A serene spa combined with a skilled technician is the best medicine for easing tension. Suggest to the bride that she schedule a treatment to relax her on the day of her wedding, such as a massage, a body wrap, or a soothing moisturizing treatment. Advise her not to try anything that could adversely react with her skin, however, like an intense facial or a waxing.

Take Charge

She's got enough to worry about just getting ready for this shindig. If she's stressing about the arrival of the photographer, the flowers, and the rest of the bridesmaids, make phone calls on her behalf or delegate some of these organizational tasks. If a wedding-day emergency should arise, try to make as little fuss as possible about it and to solve the problem without the bride's involvement. Then help her put on her crinoline, protect her dress from her freshly made-up face, and give her any last-minute beauty touchups.

Provide Water and Snacks

No doubt nerves will prompt the bride to claim she doesn't feel like eating. And whether she's truly too stressed to eat or she's trying to avoid gaining that last extra ounce, it is very important that she has a small meal or a few light snacks (at the very least) in the hours leading up to her wedding.

Prepare a snack of healthful fruits and cheese, crackers, or whatever you think she'll be likely to eat, so she won't become lightheaded or feel weak as the day goes on. And when you get to the reception, bring her a special plate of crudités and hors d'oeuvres during the cocktail hour. She'll be so busy mingling that she won't have the time or inclination seek them out herself.

Also be sure to keep plenty of water readily available all day in order to stay hydrated, especially if it's a hot summer day. Keep a small cooler of spring water in your limo or car for everyone to access.

Be Her Breathing Coach

The butterflies will surely hit right before she walks down the aisle. To alleviate the physical symptoms, including shaking, a racing heart, or lungs that can't seem to get enough air, advise her to breathe deeply. Like a Lamaze coach, breathe with her, and count to ten with deep breaths.

Create an Atmosphere of Calm as You're Getting Ready

Set up aromatherapy candles. Play some light, relaxing music. Dim the lights. Close the door to the chaos of family members, children, or other bridesmaids. Sensory overload can affect even the calmest of brides, so try to tune out the stressful effects of hyper kids, loud music, or overindulgent relatives as the bride attempts to get ready.

FACT

Stress need not play a big part in the wedding day, for you or for the bride. By now, all the plans should be in motion—and if they're not, there's nothing you can really do about it anyway. Make an effort to chill out and just enjoy the day.

Get Goofy

It's all so serious–putting on the dress, perfecting the makeup, keeping every hair in place. The ride to the ceremony site (or waiting to walk down the aisle) can be especially tense, as the bride visualizes the impending scene in her head and realizes that this is what all her hard work has been leading up to.

Break the tension by doing something unexpected, like initiating a sing-along, a game of charades, a burping contest–whatever you think will make the bride laugh. Do whatever it takes to relieve the buildup of tension, particularly during the hour leading up to the ceremony.

Spare the Details

Don't upset the bride with any bad news. Whether it's bad news from the outside world, or something that's gone wrong with a wedding vendor or family member, no good will come of telling her difficult news in the hour before the wedding.

Reassure Her That She Looks Stunning

Tell her she's never looked more beautiful. That she's gonna rock her fiancé's world the minute he sees her. Tell her whatever it takes to allay any fears that she looks less than perfect.

Plan for Contingencies

To prepare for smaller bridal emergencies, pack a go-to kit in advance with the following enclosed: safety pins, stain removers, small hairbrush and comb, aspirin, heartburn medication, tampon, panty liners, breath mints, pen and paper, sunscreen, bottled water, and dental floss.

By providing a mental port for the bride's prewedding storm, you really have an opportunity to show off your bridesmaid skills. While she may not ask for your help outright, utilizing these subtle, behind-the-scenes methods will help you ease her mind—and maybe your own in the process. And that brings us to our next topic.

De-Stressing Yourself

In all of your efforts to calm the bride, you mustn't forget to give yourself a little TLC, too. It's only natural that you, too, may be feeling the pressure of walking down the aisle before hundreds of people you may or may not know. To minimize your worries and present a calm, cool, and collected face to the world come time for the ceremony, heed the following advice.

Do Whatever It Is That Helps You Relax

Take a long run or power walk. Do yoga. Read a book. Watch television. Bake cookies. The point is, if you've got extra time on your hands on the day of the wedding, avoid stress-causing situations. Don't call your mother if you know you'll end up in an argument. Avoid high-traffic areas of town. Don't pick a fight with your boyfriend if it can wait until Monday. You understand.

Prepare in Advance

Don't count on completing any vital tasks on the wedding day. In other words, don't wait until the last minute to do even seemingly quick and easy tasks, like purchasing a pair of pantyhose or pressing your dress. To avoid any last-minute crises, complete all your critical tasks in the days leading up to the wedding.

You'll be nervous enough without the added complications of a store that's unexpectedly closed, or a dress that's stained or damaged from ironing.

Don't Schedule Anything Major on the Day of the Wedding

Try not to venture into situations that might take an unexpected twist, such as driving to an unfamiliar destination or relying on public transportation without a healthy cushion of extra time. You can't control factors like weather and traffic, so it's best to prepare for the worst.

Follow Similar Stress-Relieving Techniques as the Bride

Take a long bath. Light a candle. Throw in the new Norah Jones CD. Get a spa treatment. And don't forget to eat something and drink plenty of fluids, so you'll have your strength and mental capacity for all the socializing, dancing, and celebrating ahead.

The Ceremony

Most wedding officiants insist on holding a ceremony rehearsal one to two days before the wedding, at which the bride, groom, parents, and the wedding party can learn exactly where they need to be and what they need to do at the ceremony—before the ceremony actually occurs.

Because most weddings have slight style variations, this rehearsal time can prove extremely valuable. For example, some officiants will direct groomsmen to meet the bridesmaids before they reach the end of the aisle, while others may direct groomsmen to hold their places near the groom until the end of the ceremony.

There are many more small, seemingly inconsequential details that you'll review, and these will become absolutely vital as hundreds of eyes fall on you during the actual ceremony. Thus, the rehearsal is a valuable time to pay attention and do what you're told, so try to save your daydreams about that incredibly gorgeous groomsman for later.

ESSENTIAL

As boring as it may seem, pay attention to the officiant at the wedding rehearsal. You definitely want to be as prepared as possible for the next day's events.

So what should you expect at the ceremony? What, specifically, will your role be and how can you best fulfill it?

Ironically, most the bridesmaid work is done by the time the ceremony takes place. All the shower planning, bachelorette-party planning, bride hand-holding, errand-running, and moral supporting will be history by the time you reach that ceremony site, at which point your duties are largely ceremonial. If you're the maid of honor, you have some specific, tangible tasks to perform, such as signing the marriage license and participating in the ring ceremony; but as a regular bridesmaid, you'll really just have to smile, look pretty, and have fun.

The Longest Aisle

Your first obvious public role as bridesmaid will be your walk down the aisle. At the rehearsal, you will learn the order of your descent, which is often based on height–shortest bridesmaids followed by taller ones. The last wedding attendant to walk down the aisle is the maid of honor. Or, if there is a flower girl, she will immediately precede the bride, throwing rose petals in her path.

As you walk down the aisle, all eyes will fall on you. This can certainly be disconcerting, especially if the spotlight is not something you enjoy. However, it will be over before you know it. The following tips will help you make the walk with grace under pressure.

Smile

If you feel weird smiling at nothing in particular, don't worry–it will look a lot weirder if you're stone-faced or frowning. For added inspiration to flash those pearly whites, make eye contact with a friendly face in the congregation. Give him or her a smile and make it last.

Stand Up Straight

As your mother always admonished, don't slouch. Walk tall and you'll exude confidence.

Walk Slowly

The most common bridesmaid offense is walking down the aisle at warp speed. Take your time and walk elegantly, at a slow pace. Even if it feels too slow, it's probably not.

Look Great to Feel Comfortable

If you think you look your best, you'll feel more comfortable when your walk down the aisle makes you the center of attention. That means ensuring your dress fits properly (not too tight or too loose, or you'll fidget with it), your hair and makeup are looking good, and that you're wearing the right undergarments. This can't be overstated.

The proper underwear makes a big difference on a long, pressure-filled day like this one. Don't wear a bra that needs constant readjustment (or one whose straps keep threatening exposure). Don't get stuck in too-tight or too-short pantyhose, and be sure your slip is the right fit and the proper length.

If you're wearing new shoes, break them in before the wedding day so they're more comfortable on your feet and so there's some wear in the soles—there are few greater wedding-day hazards than slippery new shoes on a smooth aisle runner or carpeting. Wear them around the house so they'll be comfortable and safe for walking come the wedding day.

ESSENTIAL

Be sure you've thought about what you'll be wearing *under* your dress before the big day. Wear (or purchase) a bra that will provide enough support—and won't show—under your dress. And be sure to choose hosiery in the correct size.

Keep Your Eyes Looking Forward and Your Head Steady

An occasional glance to your right and your left is fine, but move your head and eyes too much and you'll risk some strange expressions in the ensuing photo proofs. Not that it's all about the pictures, of course.

We're Here . . . Now What?

Though you've rehearsed it the night before, the ceremony will still hold some surprises—particularly how long it may feel. That's because you've probably only rehearsed the recessional and processional—not the entire ceremony. And while the average wedding ceremony lasts only an hour—a reasonable amount of time, surely—it's also an hour during which you'll still find yourself front and center, where good behavior is a must.

ALERT!

Avoid bringing extra attention to yourself during the ceremony—which means stifling that laugh and refraining from fidgeting or looking around.

At some ceremonies, the bridesmaids will be provided a row of seats in which to relax during the majority of the ceremony, but at other ceremonies you'll be expected to stand throughout. And while an hour of standing may not seem like a lot, it can become pretty tiring, especially if you're balancing on new high heels in front of a hundred or more people.

But whether you're standing or sitting, you should try to be on your best behavior, so as not to distract guests from the ceremony proceedings. Don't move around too much or fidget. If seated, do not pivot around to check out who's there. Do not poke the bridesmaid next to you when the groom flubs his lines. Do not begin laughing when the best man trips during the ceremony.

And by all means, do *not* talk. If you find yourself overtaken by a case of the giggles—precisely because you are forbidden to do so—think of something sad to calm yourself, like the fact that Matt Damon will probably never be your boyfriend.

During the Ceremony

Unless you are the maid of honor, which means you'll be assisting the bride with straightening her train, holding her bouquet, or participating in the ring ceremony, you'll have little to do besides sit (or stand) and watch as the ceremony unfolds.

Depending on the ceremony's religious rituals or traditions, you may be greeted individually by the bride and groom during a sign of peace interlude, or you may be required to take communion (if you so desire). But aside from these specific rituals, there's little to do besides be an observant guest, like those seated behind you.

After the Ceremony

Of course, you'll spring right back into action after the groom kisses his bride, smashes the glass, or helps the bride jump the broom—whatever cultural or religious ritual signifies the end of their particular ceremony. You will have reviewed at the rehearsal what to do during the recessional (you walk back down the aisle).

Most likely, at the head of the aisle, you will meet your "partner" groomsman, who will offer his arm to escort you to the back of the ceremony site. The wedding party will immediately follow the bride and groom, and no doubt there will be much music and photo flashing as you make your way to the back of the ceremony site. For this walk, you can be much more relaxed and natural. You may greet guests if you wish as you pass them on your way out.

Once you've reached the back of the church or synagogue (or wherever the ceremony's taken place), the bride may ask that you participate in a receiving line. The receiving line is just what it sounds like—a lineup of the bride, groom, their parents, and the wedding party, who greet guests as they exit the ceremony. As an alternate plan, the receiving line may also be formed to greet guests as they enter the reception. This is usually the case if there is a time delay between the ceremony and reception or if the ceremony and reception are at different locations.

If there is a receiving line, and you're not included, you'll have a few minutes to relax and unwind before the next phase of the wedding. If you're feeling productive, you may wish to help organize the bride and groom's traditional exit from the ceremony site, by passing out the "rice" (usually birdseed now, as raw rice can injure birds trying to ingest it), bubbles, or flower petals (or anything else the guests will be tossing in celebration).

ESSENTIAL

In some cases, the bride may wish to keep her receiving line moving more quickly and efficiently, in which case the bridesmaids and groomsmen won't be included in the receiving line (though the maid of honor and best man will probably still participate).

Immediately before the bride and groom exit the site, help line up guests on either side of the door to greet the bride and groom as they emerge as husband and wife for the first time. Their exit is usually followed by more mingling outside the ceremony site (unless it's raining or snowing).

If you're on a tight time schedule, as you will be if you have loads of pictures to take before you get to the reception, you can help organize your group's exit. Gracefully usher the bride and groom away from enthusiastic guests and toward the photo site or the limousine that will take them there.

The Photo Shoot

There's no escaping it. While everyone else is enjoying cocktail hour after the ceremony, the wedding party, bride, groom, and their families will be stuck posing for formal pictures. If you're lucky, the bride may have knocked off some of the required photos before the ceremony by posing for pictures with her bridesmaids in advance. No matter what, though, you'll still have plenty of posing and waiting before you can move on to the fun of the reception.

What exactly should you expect from the photo shoot? Usually, the photographer will have a long list of formal portraits to take. This list has been prepared in advance by the bride, and it will include varying configurations of people, such as the following:

- The bride with all her bridesmaids
- The bride with each bridesmaid individually
- The bride, the groom, and her bridesmaids
- The bride, the groom, her bridesmaids, and his groomsmen
- The bridesmaids and groomsmen alone

Of course, for the bride this list will be much longer, to include various configurations of family members from each side of the family. Often, the bride and groom will complete their list of formal shots with the bridal party, and then they will set you free to celebrate as they pose for portraits on their own.

Photo Shoot Celebration

Hopefully, the bride has planned a slight lag between the ceremony and reception so that you all won't miss too much of the celebration. Of course, you may wish to plan your own little photo shoot celebration, too, with some celebratory cocktails handy for an immediate post-ceremony toast.

Ask one of the groomsmen to bring a "portable bar" in the limo or to the photo site (like a cooler of white wine, champagne, beer, and so on) so you can all enjoy a wedding party cocktail as you pose for pics. It'll definitely make the photo shoot go much faster.

Girls on Film

Do you dread the thought of formal portraits because you feel you're simply not photogenic? Anyone can improve their percentages (of good photos to bad) by heeding the following tips.

Get a Good Night's Sleep

Nothing ruins your look more certainly than tired-looking eyes or a saggy, bloated face caused by lack of sleep or worse, a hangover. Unlike men, women can at least allay some of the damage with makeup. Still, it's amazing how the camera picks up imperfections you won't even notice in the mirror.

Look Your Best

Having your hair professionally styled and your makeup professionally applied can go a long way toward taking great pictures. This is particularly true if you don't regularly wear makeup. A too-pale face can cause you to look washed out in photos.

Touch Up Immediately Before You Take Pictures

Take care of those stray hairs coming loose or that spinach stuck in your teeth. Reapply lipstick, and make sure your bra strap isn't showing. A last-minute look in the mirror is insurance against photo mishaps. Carry a small compact, some pressed powder, lipstick, and lip gloss in your wedding-day bag to ensure you look fresh for photos all day long.

FACT

Study photos of yourself that you've liked in the past. Figure out the common denominators—was your hair styled a certain way? Was your body positioned at a certain angle? Use this fact-finding mission to ensure you look your best in the formal portraits.

Show Off Your Best Angle

Don't know what it is? Examine other pictures you've liked of yourself. Look at which side of your face is pictured, what position your body is in, where your arms and hands fall, and how your hair is styled. For example, you'll always look trimmer if you turn your body at a slight angle toward the camera, rather than letting yourself be photographed straight on. In addition, your face probably has a more flattering side for photographs, and even the angle at which you hold your head can make a big difference. So try to jockey for a position that flatters. (Of course, do so subtly and within reason. The photographer won't be too sympathetic to your specific needs if he's trying to organize twelve people in one shot.)

Stand or Sit Up Straight

Slouching and poor posture will definitely show up in photos. Straighten your back and lift your shoulders for the most flattering pose.

Smile

There's nothing like a big smile to make you look great on film. Think of something that makes you happy–your new boyfriend, your dog, your Hello Kitty collection–to elicit a big natural smile right before the photographer snaps.

The Reception

Finally, it's time to relax and really celebrate. The most common type of wedding reception begins in the early evening with a cocktail hour, followed by a meal, followed by dancing. Interspersed are a number of time-honored traditions that you, as bridesmaid, may also be a part of.

Generally, your duties now lie strictly in celebrating and having fun. By virtue of your telltale dress you'll still stand out among the other wedding guests, so try to behave as the bride's goodwill emissary even after your duties have officially ended. Because you'll still attract attention as the evening progresses, save the dirty dancing, heavy drinking, and chain smoking for another evening (or at least for the after-hours party).

FACT

Even though the ceremony's over, your bridesmaid duties may not be. Be prepared to take part in reception traditions that may include the bouquet toss, the wedding party dance, and more.

You don't want to create any mini-scandals at this family event, and you don't want to be forever known for inappropriate behavior among people who've never even met you. This happened to one Jacksonville, Florida, bridesmaid who drank too much on an empty stomach and didn't make it to the bathroom quite in time when the nausea hit.

As you can imagine, this unfortunate incident made quite a splash (no pun intended) among the wedding guests, who tittered and gossiped about it all evening. And the groom's family, who had never met her before, will always remember her for this dramatic first impression, rather than her great smile or successful law career.

But aside from being on your best behavior, what are your more tangible duties as the reception unfolds? Obviously every wedding is different. Not every bride will include every tradition in her wedding, and some brides will add new ones. This section covers some of the more common wedding-day traditions that you can expect to include you.

The Formal Introduction

There is a practice at some weddings that immediately follows cocktail hour and immediately precedes the serving of the meal, when everyone is seated. This is the formal announcement of the bridal party and the bride and groom to the rest of the wedding guests.

If you thought your role in the spotlight was over after you journeyed down the aisle, you're not finished yet–you will once again have to walk into a room with all eyes on you. Typically, the DJ or band emcee will announce each member of the bridal party, including groomsmen, bridesmaids, the best man, and the maid of honor. When your name is announced, you will enter the reception room and walk to your seat.

Bridal Party Seating

So where *will* you be sitting, anyway? If the wedding calls for a traditional seating plan, expect to sit at a long head table with seating on one side only. Seated at the table will be the bride and groom, the maid of honor and best man, and the bridesmaids and groomsmen. Often this table is raised on a platform so guests can better view the wedding party. Traditionally, seating is boy/girl with the bride and groom at the center, the maid of honor next to the groom, the best man next to the bride, and so on until everyone is seated. Typically, children in the bridal party are seated elsewhere, with their parents.

FACT

The traditional "head table" is the table at which the bride, groom, and bridal party are seated for dinner. It is usually a long, rectangular table at which you'll be seated only on one side, facing outward toward the wedding guests.

This traditional seating plan has loosened in recent years, however. And while many weddings still adhere to it, other couples are choosing to adopt alternative seating arrangements.

Some brides find that round tables earmarked for the wedding party are more social, as is seating the wedding party with their dates or spouses (instead of across the room from them, which often happens when the traditional head table is used). This is wholly dependent on the preferences of the bride and groom, and you probably won't know your seating arrangement until you actually arrive at the reception and pick up your place card.

Of course, some weddings don't have formal seating at all. The cocktail-style or station-style wedding may feature a smaller number of reception tables that are meant to seat guests on a sporadic basis, rather than all at once. This type of wedding is designed to promote mingling and dancing over sitting at one table for a long length of time. There are no place cards, so you'll largely be on your own.

Bridal Party Dance

Another tradition that seems to be losing some of its old-time popularity is the bridal party dance. This dance among the wedding party typically follows the bride's dance with her father.

If the bride chooses to incorporate this tradition, you'll be expected to dance to one song with your groomsman "partner" while all the guests look on. This groomsman is typically the one who escorted you up the aisle following the wedding ceremony. Perhaps he's someone you've been waiting to dance with all night . . . but if he's not, be polite and courteous. This is tradition, after all—you don't have to go home with the guy.

Fortunately, you'll be sharing the spotlight with the rest of the wedding party, so if you're best characterized by two left feet, there's still a chance no one will notice. Of course, you may also use this tradition as an excuse to take those dance lessons at the local Y or dance studio—especially if you know in advance that your dance partner is actually someone you care to impress.

Bridal Party Toasts

Traditionally, the best man and the father of the bride offer wedding day toasts, and they are sometimes also joined by the father of the groom. But in recent years this tradition, too, has loosened, and more and more honored guests are offering up a few words, particularly the maid of honor.

If the floor seems open to multiple toasts, you, too, may wish to take the opportunity to say a few words. Or, if you'd prefer a smaller, more intimate crowd, you may also consider offering your toast/speech at the rehearsal dinner. If you do plan to add a few words at the wedding reception, be sure to let the bride or groom know in advance, so that they can alert the emcee or DJ to pass the mike to you at the appropriate time.

FACT

If you plan to offer a wedding-day or rehearsal dinner toast, prepare in advance. Write it down or memorize it, and you'll be more confident and assured when you deliver it.

The best toasts are short and to the point. You may want to tell a funny anecdote, a sentimental story, or just offer your best wishes on behalf of the bridesmaids.

The Bouquet Toss

No wedding event is more universally symbolized in movies, soap operas, or chick lit than the (oft-dreaded) bouquet toss. This tradition, once a benign practice meant to symbolize the bride's goodwill toward the bridesmaids, is today often viewed with dread. But why does a seemingly innocent tradition, in which the bride tosses her bouquet to the unattached female guests, cause so much controversy?

Bouquet Toss Controversy

First, the tradition's very nature separates female guests into those who are engaged or married from those who are single. And as we well know, this is often a touchy subject.

Many unattached women may not wish to be "singled" out publicly, especially if they're sensitive about their marital status. Some women simply feel this practice is loaded with negative symbolism, by placing her entire gender in a clamoring position to be the next one married.

Of course, some women simply view the bouquet toss as a harmless, fun tradition that shouldn't be taken so seriously. Especially those under the age of fifteen, who think it's great fun.

No matter what your feelings about the tradition, however, you are among the most recognizable female guests at the wedding. As such, you are expected to be at the center of this tradition (unless you're married, that is). If the bride chooses to include the bouquet toss, be enthusiastic and lighthearted about it. (Or, if you simply can't stomach it, now may be a good time to locate that powder room.)

Garter Toss

The bouquet toss tradition is also sometimes extended to include the men, with a "brother" tradition called the garter toss. First, the groom makes a lighthearted show of removing the bride's garter from beneath her wedding dress. Then, the groom tosses the garter over his shoulder, to be caught by one of the single male guests who've assembled behind him. Then, the lucky grabber of the garter places the garter onto the leg of the woman who's caught the bouquet—while the guests look on.

Yes, there is historical significance to this practice, which stems back a couple hundred years. Superstition held that a woman presented with another bride's garter would remain faithful to the man who gave it to her.

Obviously, not every woman will enjoy a stranger moving up, up, up her thigh with a garter in a public forum, which is probably another reason women have begun avoiding the bouquet toss in recent years. But it is all in fun, and it's a long-held tradition. Again, if you find yourself in this situation, try to make light of it and enjoy the attention. Give the garter guy a hard time, and make a funny show of it. Guests will appreciate the sense of humor on that cute, sassy bridesmaid who caught the bouquet.

After-Hours

Of course, the party ain't over 'til it's over. After most weddings, you'll usually find a group of stragglers willing to forge ahead, celebrating even more. If the bride and groom are among them, more power to them—they don't want this party to end, and why should they, really?

After all, you only get married once—well, half the people do, anyway. Whether the newlyweds are in attendance or not, heed the following tips when signing on for after-hours.

Go Home, or Close to Home

Invite guests back to your house or the hotel bar (or hotel room, if it's large enough). Don't start bar-hopping unless you have prearranged transportation, like cabs or a limo.

Prearrange for Some Drinks and Snacks

Buy a few bottles of wine or champagne in advance, and have some bottled water, coffee, and snacks available for those who wish to sober up. In addition, check with the caterer to see if you can take home any leftover liquor from the wedding—often, once a bottle is open, it's paid for, and otherwise it may go to waste.

Don't Harass the Bride and Groom

This is often a favorite pastime of wedding guests under the influence, and in fact is a reason why many newlyweds keep their hotel whereabouts a secret. Even if it's all in good fun, the bride and groom have better things to do than endure your attention, even if it's just catching up on some sleep before their honeymoon.

Be Mentally Prepared for the Next Day

After many weddings, you'll be invited to attend a post-wedding brunch or a party at someone's home as a final sendoff before the wedding weekend is over. Exhaustion or a hangover won't make you enjoy it anymore. In fact, either factor could make a brunch (and potential travel home afterward) akin to torture. Try to get to bed relatively early, and drink lots of water before dozing off.

Great Gifts

The wedding day wouldn't be complete without giving a gift to the bride and groom. But what should you get, and how much should you spend? This is a very personal decision. And different regions of the country have different standards of "normal." For example, what's normal in New York City may seem extravagant in the Midwest (and conversely, what's normal in the Midwest may seem cheap in NYC). Of course, anyone who's judging your wedding gift solely by the amount you've spent is materialistic and difficult to satisfy anyway, so the bottom line is this—give from your heart, and give only what you can afford.

But what should that item be? A toaster? A blender? A set of silver? Or something more creative? Obviously, that's up to you. Your only real criterion is to give something you believe the bride and groom will appreciate and find useful.

And the first rule of gift-giving is to choose not only what *you* like, but what you think *they'll* like. Which means to try to walk in their shoes. Don't buy them a martini set if they don't drink. Don't give them an ultra-contemporary vase if they prefer classic design. And if they really just want a lot of practical, everyday items, skip the crystal.

QUESTION?

Do I have to choose a wedding gift from the bridal registry?

No. By choosing something from the registry, however, you'll be sure to give a gift the bride and groom will find useful. But you may also feel compelled to give something more personal and original. Ultimately, the choice is yours.

The following are some creative wedding gift ideas for brides and grooms with all kinds of tastes and interests:

- A piece of art that reflects the ceremony or reception site
- A gift certificate to a great restaurant near their honeymoon destination
- A gift certificate to Home Depot (if they've just bought a house)
- Tickets to an upcoming concert, sporting event, or art exhibit

- Membership to a beer-of-the-month, steak-of-the-month, or other specialty club
- An extravagant item they'll have forever, such as a Tiffany clock, a beautiful crystal bowl, silver chopsticks, etc.
- Something you've made (knit them a blanket, make them a quilt, create a set of pottery—wherever your talents lie)
- A remote car starter (great for cold climates)
- A car CD player
- Hobby-related gifts: ski lift passes to a nearby resort, his and hers tennis rackets, boating accessories, camping gear, three seasons of *The Sopranos* on DVD.
- A cool gadget from a specialty store or catalog (Pick out something that you know they'd want but never get for themselves.)
- A case of a wine
- A state-of-the-art bottle opener
- An extravagant salt and pepper shaker
- A gift certificate to a local hotel and restaurant for a mini-getaway
- His and hers massages
- A mailbox for their new home
- A safe (put something fun inside to surprise them)
- A gift certificate for a home cleaning service

Above all, remember to have fun and cherish the wedding day. You'll have great memories to look back on.

Chapter 9
Special Circumstances

Not every wedding is movie perfect. Really, even most movie weddings aren't movie perfect. After all, without all the drama, what fun is there? Real life always gets in the way of perfection, and even under the most ideal conditions (huge budgets, cooperative families) there's the potential that something will go awry. Here are some of the things you may be faced with, and what you need to know to deal with each situation without losing sight of the main goal.

Always the Diplomat

As a bridesmaid, you should be aware of some of the unusual circumstances–or potential pitfalls–that might make your role a little murky. Under most circumstances, your responsibilities as bridesmaid will remain the same, but there are some situations that may prompt you to do things a little differently. This chapter covers the full gamut of unexpected or unusual circumstances that may arise during the wedding you're participating in.

Second Weddings

There's nothing unusual about a second wedding. In fact, four out of ten weddings in the United States are the second wedding for one or both partners. The only unusual aspect about them is that they may incorporate philosophies or practices that could alter your role as a "traditional" bridesmaid, though even that is not a foregone conclusion. In recent years, second weddings have become more and more like first weddings, rather than the quieter, more intimate events of the past.

FACT

Second weddings account for approximately 40 percent of all U.S. weddings. While they're not uncommon, there are some special considerations for you as bridesmaid—such as whether to throw a shower and a bachelorette party.

Is It Any Different?

Obviously, just like every first wedding is different, so is every second wedding. There's no way to lump them into one category, or to predict what tone any individual party will take.

Ultimately, it will be up to the bride and groom to determine what style wedding they have. Some brides may choose to pull out all the stops, including the big white dress, the big white cake, and the huge guest list—especially if they didn't have it the first time around.

Other brides, though, may feel that a large, elaborate wedding is inappropriate, impractical, or too similar to their first weddings. In this case, they may wish to have a less formal tone, fewer guests, or a simpler ceremony. If the bride plans on holding a scaled-down affair, your wedding-day duties may be significantly fewer, too, with a loosening of certain traditions. As with any wedding, follow the bride's lead for guidance.

In general, you should treat this wedding just as you would a bride's first wedding. It's no less special or meaningful an occasion, and if you've agreed to be a bridesmaid, you've agreed to all the formalities that go with it.

But what about those prewedding responsibilities, like planning the shower and bachelorette party? Are these parties even appropriate for a second wedding, and if so, are the bridesmaids still responsible for hosting them?

Showers

The answer to these questions depends on the individual bride. From an etiquette perspective, a shower is a perfectly appropriate occasion for a second wedding. As such, the maid of honor and bridesmaids have a duty to plan one, if the bride so desires.

ESSENTIAL

Before you begin planning a shower or bachelorette party for a bride's second wedding, determine her comfort level. There's a possibility she may not want a lot of hoopla for either event.

There may be brides, however, who wish not to have a shower. Perhaps she's uncomfortable about being on the receiving end of gifts again, for instance, especially if her first wedding wasn't far in the past. If this is the case, but you'd still like to honor the bride by bringing her close family and friends together before the wedding, you can still plan a "no gifts" party, or specify a charity for donations in lieu of gifts.

Bachelorette Parties

But what about a bachelorette party? Again, the bride should make her wishes known on the topic. Some second-time brides may feel one bachelorette party in a lifetime is plenty, while others may crave all the fun and excitement that surrounded their first wedding. This will largely depend on the bride's specific circumstances and her personality.

As with any wedding, you should follow the bride's lead regarding the other elements of being a bridesmaid. But there's a good chance that she may be more relaxed about wedding-day decisions such as what you'll wear. Perhaps she'll let you choose your own dress or give you some easy parameters such as a color and length. Or maybe she'll choose a dress but go easy on demands for shoes, jewelry, and so on.

Gender Benders

Another growing trend in recent years is being a bridesmaid . . . for the groom. Many marrying couples have close relationships that cross gender barriers, and they wouldn't dream of excluding close friends or family members from participating in the wedding simply because they're not the same sex. Thus, more women are serving in the wedding party for the groom, and more men are serving for the bride.

What Would I Wear?

Certainly, this does not mean that men have to don a bridesmaid dress and women have to rent a tux (though the woman-in-tux thing is a little easier to digest). Usually, a woman who's close with the groom will wear the same outfit as the bridesmaids, and a man serving for the bride will wear whatever the groomsmen are wearing.

This can lead to questions. For instance, just because you'll be dressed as a bridesmaid (but are technically a groomsman), does it mean you have to act as one, with all the traditional shower-planning and bachelorette-hosting duties that go with it? Will you be invited to the bachelor party? How, exactly, will this whole thing work?

How Will It Work?

Very likely, if the bride and groom have included you as an unconventional bridesmaid, they've thought out all the contingencies. Which means that with any luck, you can simply refer to them with any uncertainties. Perhaps they'll decide against having gender-specific parties, preferring a coed shower and mixed bachelor/bachelorette party, especially if they both have a mixed social circle. Or maybe they have no interest in these traditional conventions anyway, in which case you won't have to worry at all.

ALERT!

If you're serving as "bridesmaid" for the groom, keep the lines of communication open. When in doubt about your duties, ask.

There is a chance, however, that you'll be lumped in with the rest of the bridesmaids. Probably you would have been invited to these events anyway, as a close friend of the groom's. But does that mean you have to help plan and pay for all of them?

There's no real clear-cut answer to this question, and no formal etiquette that dictates what to do in this scenario. If the maid of honor is contacting you with the details, you'll probably be expected to participate. If she hasn't contacted you, it probably means she's treating you as if you were a traditional groomsman (which, aside from the dress—and your gender—you are).

A generous and thoughtful gesture would be for you to offer your help to the rest of the bridesmaid troupe, especially if you have developed a relationship with the bride. If you've never met her (and by extension, her bridesmaids), your participation might feel a bit more awkward. Like Julia Roberts's character in *My Best Friend's Wedding,* suddenly becoming the bride's new best friend might be odd—even if she's as sweet as Cameron Diaz's character. And especially if you're in love with the groom—which of course you aren't, right?

What Should I Do?

No matter what, your best bet is always to err on the side of caution. It never hurts to offer assistance, and you'll figure out soon enough if your help is wanted or not. When all else fails, simply communicate your questions or uncertainty to the groom. He, too, should offer guidance regarding how he'd like the situation to work, especially when it comes to attending that bachelor party. Just beware if he tells you that one of your duties is jumping out of the cake.

The Wedding That Never Happened

You can hardly believe it. Two weeks before the wedding, it's been canceled. And while you may or may not know the reasons yet, there's one thing you definitely *don't* know–and that's what to do next.

What's the Situation?

Needless to say, this is a situation your mother would gingerly label as "difficult"–a vast understatement from the bride's perspective, surely, but appropriate for just about everyone else. No doubt the bride is completely devastated, even if it was she who ultimately called it off. There may have been dramatic circumstances initiating their breakup, or perhaps it was long in coming.

Or maybe they didn't break up at all, but simply postponed the wedding until an undetermined date. No matter what the circumstances, this couple's problems will unfortunately be subject to the public eye, due to the widely announced impending nuptials.

ESSENTIAL

If the wedding is canceled, your most important duty as bridesmaid is to lend an ear—or a shoulder to cry on. The bride will undoubtedly need a great deal of moral support, whether it was her decision to cancel or not.

Show Your Support

So before you consider your own circumstances as canceled bridesmaid, try to consider your friend, the bride. Not only is the relationship with the man she loves suffering (or over), but it's also happened in a very public forum. In addition to her sadness about the relationship, she's probably also feeling guilty and embarrassed about canceling the wedding.

That said, try to be a supportive, helpful friend. Don't call her the next day to find out what you should do with your bridesmaid dress. Don't ask her whether the store will take back your shoes. And don't inquire about returning the shower gift you gave her. In other words, don't make her feel worse than she already does. There will be plenty of time once things have calmed down to take care of practical matters. Your job now, as a bridesmaid (and a friend) is to offer a shoulder to cry on and plenty of moral support.

The Practical Matters

So what about those practical issues? If you can't bother the bride about them, what should you do?

Again, that depends on the circumstances. If the wedding's simply been postponed, not canceled, hang on to your dress and all the accoutrements until further notice. But if it has been officially canceled, keep the dress for a suitable period of time—a month or two—then decide what to do with it.

With few exceptions, most bridal shops will not accept returns on wedding or bridesmaid dresses. So, your only other option is to keep it, if you think you'll wear it to some other occasion, or to sell it through a consignment shop, a classified ad, or online at an auction site like eBay.

Of course, if you think there's any chance the wedding will be rescheduled as originally planned, don't sell the dress, or you may have to buy another one at full price again.

FACT

If the wedding's been canceled very close to the wedding date, you may wish to offer your help to the bride's family writing notes or making phone calls to inform invited guests about the cancellation.

If you've already sent a wedding gift, you should expect to receive it back. In addition, etiquette dictates that the bride should return all engagement and shower gifts to the gift-giver, provided they have not been used. Again, if the bride is slow to take care of these practical issues, cut her some slack. Or offer your help to package and send items back to the gift-givers, if you think she'd welcome it.

Keeping Perspective

While it's natural to feel resentful that you've spent so much time, effort, and money on an event that never happened, keep things in perspective. While you may be out a few bucks, the bride is out a fiancé, not to mention her entire idea of the future. And it was never her intention to dupe you or the many other loving friends and family with whom she celebrated her engagement.

You may also wish to prepare some answers in advance for probing third parties. Neither the bride nor you are obligated to explain to anyone why the wedding has been canceled. When questioned, use your discretion, and look to the bride to determine how much information to give. She may prefer that most of the details remain private, no matter what the circumstances of the cancellation.

The Theme Wedding

While certainly less stressful than many possible wedding-day scenarios, a theme wedding may inspire certain questions that a traditional, straightforward wedding celebration doesn't.

In case you need a reminder, a theme wedding is an event that incorporates an overriding idea or concept into the wedding ceremony and/or reception. Popular themes include Renaissance or medieval weddings, Victorian weddings, and holiday-themed weddings (Christmas, New Year's, and Valentine's Day are popular ones). Also included are traditional ethnic weddings, which bring back rituals and practices from the "old country" into modern wedding celebrations.

Because these alternative-style weddings have grown in popularity in recent years, there's a chance that the wedding in which you're participating may be planned as a theme wedding. Read ahead to find out what to expect.

FACT

For a theme wedding, you may be asked to don some creative duds. Think of it as an adventure—at least you don't have to wear another unflattering pastel gown.

Theme Wedding Threads

Your duties probably won't change much for a theme wedding, but the way you carry them out probably will. For example, if the bride is planning a medieval theme wedding, don't expect to wear that lavender satin dress with the dyed-to-match shoes.

More likely you'll resemble the woman on the cover of your favorite historical romance bodice ripper. That means you'll be renting your bridesmaid dress at a costume shop, or the bride may have hired a seamstress to custom-make them. Regardless of where you get it or what the theme is, the standard rules still apply–you'll be responsible for purchasing and properly fitting your outfit before the wedding day.

In addition, you'll be responsible for purchasing and renting your shoes and accessories. Don't enjoy the prospect of dressing as a medieval wench, a 1920s flapper, or a Victorian-age lass? If you haven't figured it out by now, this is your lot as bridesmaid. And actually, a theme wedding may provide a nice departure from the typical, oft-unflattering bridesmaid dress.

Theme Preparties

What about showers and other preparties? Do these have to stay in theme, too? As a host, this is entirely up to you. If it's a theme you believe you can carry off, perhaps you'll enjoy incorporating it into the shower. But if it seems like an uphill effort, maybe the impact of the theme is best saved for the wedding. In fact, if you are thinking of throwing a related theme shower, you may want to okay it with the bride beforehand. She may feel it could steal the theme's thunder at the wedding.

Of course, you could always incorporate the theme into the shower or bachelorette party with just a small teaser. For example, if the bride is planning a Roaring Twenties wedding, you could throw a traditional shower in every way, but also play 1920s pop tunes at the shower, or give favors related to the era, like tiny "bootleg" bottles of liquor.

ESSENTIAL

If you want to "tease" a Christmas-themed wedding, give tree ornaments as favors, and serve holiday favorites like eggnog and Christmas cookies, even if the shower is a month or two before the big day.

Staying in Theme During the Main Event

On the wedding day itself, your duties may differ from those of the traditional bridesmaid. For very elaborate theme weddings, the ceremony and reception may differ tremendously from a traditional wedding's, or it may revive traditions from long ago. Perhaps it will mean the elimination of the traditional ceremony processional and recessional or of reception traditions like the wedding party dance or the bouquet toss. A theme wedding may also mean the addition of new rituals or traditions that you'll be expected to take part in. If so, the bride should let you know in advance, so you'll be prepared on the wedding day. If in doubt, ask her beforehand.

Personal Circumstances

Just because you're a bridesmaid doesn't mean the rest of your life stops—even if you suspect the bride sometimes wishes it would. But it does mean that sometimes your own life can get in the way of being the best bridesmaid you can be. Unfortunately, we can't always control when big or stressful life events occur. And while some factors that arise may be perfectly legitimate excuses for shirking your bridesmaid duties, others are probably just that—excuses. Consult the following list to determine the potential results of various life complications and how they reflect on you as a bridesmaid.

Dilemma: You break up with your boyfriend in the months leading up to the wedding.

Poison potential: Being a bridesmaid only exaggerates your own loneliness. In fact, you've begun despising all things couple related. You find yourself blowing off bridesmaid duties, and your cynicism is beginning to affect (and annoy) all the other bridesmaids. Plus, you dread attending the wedding dateless.

How to deal: Make being the world's best bridesmaid your personal pet project. Take all that energy you formerly spent on your boyfriend and invest it in the bride. It will not only distract you from your woes, it will help out the bride and bring you closer. At the wedding (to distract you from your solo status), keep busy with bridesmaids' tasks. And scope out the groomsmen and single male guests. Weddings are one of the best places to find that rebound guy—or better yet, something more permanent.

Dilemma: You lose your job during the engagement.

Poison potential: Your self-esteem takes a major dip, not to mention your bank account. You're worried enough about paying your gas bill without worrying about buying that pair of overpriced dyeables. You begin avoiding the bride and the other bridesmaids, hoping this commitment will somehow just go away.

How to deal: Talk to the bride. Tell her your circumstances. If she's a true friend, she'll either help you foot the bill or let you off the hook with no hard feelings. She might also let you participate on a smaller scale, like giving you a reading or other honored task to perform.

Dilemma: You move away.

Poison potential: You can barely keep track of where you packed your kitchenware, much less the details of this wedding. Between moving away from town and reorganizing your life, you've definitely been lax in your bridesmaid duties.

How to deal: Pick up the pace. While this is surely a stressful time for you, you did commit to being a bridesmaid, so do all you can to honor that commitment. Try to participate as much as you can, despite the distance. Keep in touch with the bride and bridesmaids via phone calls or e-mails. Try to attend prewedding events when possible.

Dilemma: You and the bride have a falling out.

Poison potential: Perhaps she's become Bridezilla, and you've had as much as you can stand. Or perhaps she's confronted *you* with some perceived transgression. No matter what the circumstances, bridal resentment is certainly not inspiring you to be an enthusiastic bridesmaid.

How to deal: A conflict with the bride during this emotionally charged time can be devastating to a friendship. Tread carefully. Try to face the conflict openly and get past it, however, by having a heart-to-heart with the bride. You definitely want to mend fences before the wedding, and ignoring the problem or avoiding the bride won't help matters. If you think she's acting unreasonably, try to extend your patience. The stress of the wedding may be causing her to act in ways she normally wouldn't. Presumably she'll be back to normal post-honeymoon.

Dilemma: Family obligations become overwhelming.

Poison potential: You've helped the bride with many prewedding tasks, but suddenly you've got some family obligations that demand more of your time—a grandparent who's ill, a child who needs attention, marital difficulties. And while you'd like to help more, there simply aren't enough hours in the day.

How to deal: Once again, explain your situation to the bride. And again, if she is a true friend, she'll be more than understanding. If you feel comfortable doing so, you may also wish to alert the bridesmaids about your circumstances, in case you need their help with wedding-related duties.

Dilemma: You get ill before the big day.

Poison potential: Obviously your health takes precedence over everything else in your life. But if you've fallen ill, you may be feeling guilty for not participating enough—or for knowing you won't be able to carry out your bridesmaid duties.

How to deal: If you've been struck with a temporary illness right before the wedding, such as the stomach flu, let the bride know as soon as possible. Then try to do as much as you can, such as participating in the ceremony but skipping the reception. Obviously, there may be cases when you're simply too weak to do anything. If it's a more serious, chronic condition, you should also alert the bride. She will understand if it prevents you from performing your full range of duties.

Dilemma: There's a death in your family.

Poison potential: This is a worst-case, emergency scenario.

How to deal: In the event that someone close to you becomes ill or dies immediately preceding the wedding date, you'll need to use your best judgment. Obviously, if services conflict with the wedding, you will have to skip the wedding. If you are grieving, you may also feel as if you're not up for a happy event, but keep in mind that participating may also serve as therapy. Being surrounded by close friends and/or family can alleviate your feelings of isolation. In any case, do what feels right to you.

Dilemma: There's a death in the bride's or groom's family.

Poison potential: Another worst-case scenario.

How to deal: In the unfortunate event of a death in the bride's or groom's family close to the wedding date, there's a chance the event may be canceled. If so, you may wish to offer your help to the family by calling to inform wedding guests. The bride and groom may also decide that it's best if the event went on as planned or with certain modifications. Follow the bride's lead when it comes to changes to the original plans.

Post-Wedded Bliss

Of course, unusual or unexpected circumstances can also occur *after* the wedding date. In fact, dealing with your friend as a suddenly married person is an unusual circumstance unto itself. Even if everything leading up to the wedding has gone just fine—you helped plan a great shower and an eventful bachelorette party, and you even managed to walk down the aisle with no major stumbles—there's another world to deal with beyond the wedding date. As a close friend or family member of the bride, what changes are in store now that she's insulated in wedded bliss?

ESSENTIAL

For some brides, life won't change at all once she's going by the title of "Mrs." For others, everything changes. Be aware of how this may affect your friendship.

The first year of marriage for a couple—especially two relatively young people who've never gone through it before—can be extremely stressful and difficult. This is partly because no one's bothered to think about life beyond the wedding day. Many brides are so all-consumed with wedding and honeymoon planning that they haven't stopped to think about the major changes in store, like the following.

- Leaving the security of home
- Suddenly sharing everything with their man, from the bathroom to the phone to finances
- Sleeping with someone else in her bed—every night
- Checking with her husband on major purchases and other big decisions
- Running a household
- Giving up her single-girl spontaneity and independence

Taken all at once, these changes can be a bit overwhelming, even if they are what the bride has dreamed about her whole young life. Plus, many brides experience post-wedding depression, due to the inevitable drop in activity, excitement, and attention once the engagement and honeymoon are over.

But what does this mean to you—her bridesmaid and friend? How will her marriage affect you and your friendship? It would be easy to say nothing will change, but it's more likely that her marriage will affect some aspects of your friendship, for better or worse.

Time

Whereas your weekly routine used to consist of one night a week at your place watching *Sex and the City*, and one night at hers catching the latest episode of *The Bachelor*, all of a sudden she's "too busy." Why the big blowoff?

With a new husband comes a new routine. And while she shouldn't give up on her outside interests entirely, she may need to compromise some of her old routines in the name of spending time with her husband–at least in the short term. Give her some time. If she's not back by the next television sweeps season, start laying on the guilt.

FACT

Make a genuine effort to get along with the bride's new husband. The better friends you become, the more you'll see your friend—with or without him around.

Flexibility

Those last-minute shopping trips to Manhattan may be a little more difficult to pull off now. As are the weekends in the Caribbean and cross-state road trips. Heck, even that day trip to the beach has become a struggle to plan.

The fact is that your friend and her new hubby will probably be making a wholehearted, newlywed effort to coordinate all their time off together, which means excursions with you won't be her top priority. Does this mean you've lost a travel partner? That you'll need to start jockeying for a new best friend?

We hope not forever. Even if those week-long road trips are a thing of the past, you can still try to corral her company for a weekend with the girls, or even an overnighter. The key is compromise. Try to understand that she's in the throes of newlywed bliss right now, and that this too shall pass. Be patient while she figures out how to divvy up her free time with all the people now in her life, including her husband, her family, her in-laws, and her friends.

ALERT!

The first year of marriage can be very difficult on the bride, as she settles into a new life and a new routine. This may mean your friendship will experience changes, as well. Be prepared and patient, and you'll both weather any storms.

Intimacy

You used to share every minute detail of your lives, from your latest blind dates to your sexual experiences. Now you feel she's holding back. What's up with that?

Many women feel they're betraying their husbands if they reveal the negative aspects of their marriages, like disagreements, disappointments, or other conflicts. Especially during the first year of marriage, many new brides feel as if admitting to problems means they have problem marriages, when in fact they're simply having completely normal growing pains.

And it's also normal if some of the allegiance she shared with you shifts to her husband, who has, after all, become her number-one life partner (even if you are her best friend). As difficult as it may be to deal with, her husband may become her primary confidant—a role you're used to filling.

That might hurt, but try to understand and evolve with it. You can still be just as close, even if sharing her is sometimes a drag. And try not to resent her new husband, or the problem may only become worse.

As far as the sex talk goes, once one is married (or in a serious relationship), what happens in the bedroom should generally stay in the bedroom—which means the details you used to share so openly with your friend may be a done deal. After all, would you want your future husband sharing his intimate experiences with *you* with his buddies in the locker room? These experiences should be sacred between husband and wife, and as such you should respect her privacy—even if you're used to getting all the dish.

ALERT!

Once she's married, your friendship with the bride will probably change in some ways—at least temporarily—as she adjusts to a completely new lifestyle. Try to roll with the changes and offer extra amounts of patience, and your relationship will continue to grow and evolve.

Patience

She never minded those 2 A.M. post-date phone calls before. Now she's screening her calls or blowing you off until the next day. You need a Sunday morning quarterback/date analyst *now,* not after your buzz has worn off. What's a girl to do?

Remember, your late-night phone call affects not just your friend but also her new roommate–her husband. Save it for the morning, or incur his wrath. There are new boundaries you have to learn, and this is one of them. It will do nothing but hurt your friendship with the bride if the groom dislikes you. Unfortunately, many female friendships have been known to suffer because her spouse doesn't get along with her friends.

Lifestyle

Maybe you used to head out to the clubs most weekends for a few cocktails and dancing. Or maybe you could count on her to join you for a fairly regular happy hour or weeknight dinner.

It's possible that now that she's "settled," she may forgo some of your old routines–in fact, she may have already begun doing so during the engagement period. Many women feel that once they've met the man of their dreams, they can give up the "single life" in favor of the Blockbuster night.

Again, this may be temporary. Give her some time to cocoon with her husband, and be there when she emerges–chances are it's a temporary state. And though temporary can sometimes mean a year–or two–rest assured that once she's settled into her role as wife, marital bliss will inevitably demand a taste of the old single life from time to time.

Chapter 10

Real Bridesmaids, Real Stories

As the saying goes, reality is often stranger than fiction. For some reason, that sentiment rings especially true with weddings. Maybe it's the emotion, maybe it's the money, maybe it's the extraordinary expectations, but weddings seem to bring on more than their fair share of conflicts, tragedies, and mini-disasters. Here are some real stories from real bridesmaids who have dealt with situations so outlandish they could only be true.

It Could Happen to You

The situations that follow detail some real-life dramas that involved bridesmaids just like you, who found themselves in situations ranging from unconventional to uncomfortable to out-of-control. Sometimes it was the bride. Sometimes it was the bridesmaid. And sometimes it was simply circumstance. But no matter what, they all have at least one thing in common—they actually happened. Read ahead to get the scoop on bridesmaids just like you.

Bridesmaid Foibles

Many bridesmaid mishaps are avoidable. Whether it comes to getting better organized, being more responsible, or thinking things through a little more, there are steps every bridesmaid can take to avoid stress or embarrassment on the day of the wedding. Otherwise, you may be at risk of succumbing to a variety of problems. These stories illustrate just a few of them.

The Ditzy Drinkers

Alcohol has affected every manner of bridesmaids, from the very young to the well seasoned. Unfortunately, nerves, stress, hormones, and other factors may cause what's normally an acceptable number of libations to affect a girl in the strangest of ways. There's the case of the eighteen-year-old twin sisters, both bridesmaids in their older sister's Tempe, Arizona, wedding. These underage bridesmaids planned to take full advantage of the festive status, and they had the bartender convinced they were more than old enough to partake.

Not used to imbibing more than a hard lemonade or two in one sitting, they made the unfortunate choice of ordering a variety of mixed drinks—added to a few glasses of wine at dinner. Despite a long, large dinner, they'd already done themselves in. They found themselves barely able to stand up.

Fortunately, the wedding was taking place in a hotel ballroom, so their father was able to escort them to their room with some coffee, water, and a few admonishing words, where they promptly passed out. The next day was punishment enough, when they not only had to deal with some nasty hangovers, but also became the punch line for out-of-town family and friends who gathered at the bride's family's home for a post-nuptial celebratory brunch.

ALERT!

Be careful about drinking alcohol on the day of the wedding. The nervousness and excitement of the day can cause you to drink more than you intended to, potentially ruining your day. Pace yourself, or abstain completely.

Then there's the Saratoga bridesmaid—at thirty, a seasoned partygoer (not to mention a mother of three)—who simply imbibed a little too much during the preparty festivities. With a long lag between the ceremony and the reception, the wedding party had set up a portable bar in the minibus that took them from the ceremony to the photo site to the reception. This bridesmaid had one too many bottles of fruity hooch during the photo shoot–and had to take a nap in her car during the cocktail hour. Back in time for dinner, the bride had no idea until months later, when the bridesmaid finally confessed to her absence.

And one mustn't neglect the Buffalo bridesmaid, an upstanding young woman who took full advantage of a midsummer's long, hot cocktail hour. At ninety-plus degrees in July, the air conditioning wasn't quite cutting it at this festive affair, and the guests were definitely keeping themselves refreshed with plenty of gin and tonics. This bridesmaid was no exception–she had a few too many cocktails, and not nearly enough dinner. Dizzy, and feeling a bit sick, she got a ride home, napped, and made it back in time for the band's second set–and danced up a storm. This bride never knew she was missing, either.

The moral? Pace yourself, and dinner won't be such a drag.

Forgotten Fashion

For almost four years in college, six friends spent virtually every moment together–eating meals, studying, taking classes, and going to parties. When the first of them got engaged about five years after graduation (we'll call her Muffy), they were all excited to be part of her wedding.

They knew this would be one beautiful shindig, as Muffy always did everything with great style and attention to detail. And as it turned out, her wedding was no exception. She chose beautiful bridesmaids' dresses with a black velvet top, full-skirted taupe bottom, and matching taupe shawls. The women would wear the shawls during the ceremony to cover their shoulders, which was proper for a synagogue wedding.

The bridesmaids flew into the New York City area from various parts of the country. On the morning of the wedding, two of the bridesmaids unfortunately realized they had forgotten a key part of their dresses–the shawls. Panic-stricken that they would ruin this meticulously planned affair (and without the experience of having been bridesmaids before), they considered their options. One of the bridesmaids had her mother put the shawl on the next plane to New York City (for a steep fee), and she sped out to JFK airport to pick it up. The other bridesmaid wasn't sure what to do–no one had access to her apartment, where the shawl was hanging, lonely and waiting, in her closet.

So she called the dress shop in New York where she purchased the dress, to see if they might have a sample in stock that she could borrow for the day. No luck. She then called another bridesmaid salon in the city, who told her to bring the dress in–they'd see if they could match it with something on hand. Unfortunately, they didn't have anything in stock either.

So the increasingly panicked bridesmaid had only one more choice–to try to find a piece of matching fabric that she could jerry-rig into a shawl by 7 P.M. Accompanied by her full-length dress and her very patient fiancé, she began racing around Manhattan via cab and on foot to random fabric stores, scouting out a decent match. Fifty bucks in cab fare and five pounds of lost sweat weight later, she finally found a fabric that was as close as she was going to get.

ESSENTIAL

Be sure your bridesmaid dress and all accessories are pressed and ready to go—the day *before* the wedding. You'll avoid stress and headaches from last-minute emergencies.

Late for the wedding, they raced to the hotel in Long Island and began to get ready. She figured she'd safety pin the fabric into some sort of shawl that would at least cover her shoulders. But fortunately she didn't have to–Muffy had all her bases covered. When the bridesmaids arrived at the ceremony site an hour before the wedding, they were pleased to find a seamstress from the wedding salon present for any last-minute bridal gown emergencies. Little did the seamstress know she'd be hand-sewing a shawl, but she took the shawl fabric and sewed it up like a true pro. The bride was never the wiser, and the offending bridesmaid's nerves finally calmed after her second glass of top-shelf vodka, served straight up.

The moral? Make a checklist, and check it twice. Talk to the other bridesmaids about what they're bringing, so you can help remind one another about essentials. And if you do forget something, be resourceful. Try not to worry the bride. When all else fails, realize it's really not the end of the world.

Unfortunate Circumstances

When it rains, it pours. And even though you can go months or years with nothing momentous happening in your life, you'll suddenly be hit with multiple major events, all at the same time.

Unfortunately, the world doesn't stop for any wedding (even though some brides seem to think it should). Things happen that may conflict and cause problems, and unfortunately there's often no way to predict them. As much as the bride has tried to plan a perfect event, and cover all possible contingencies, there are simply some circumstances that are impossible to predict–like illness, a family emergency, or unreasonable career demands.

Even if they're not happening to the bride, there's a whole wedding party poised for potential disasters. The following are some real-life examples of unpredictable and/or unfortunate circumstances.

The Social Butterfly

When twenty-something Dinah from Baltimore was asked to be a bridesmaid in two weddings on the same day, she wasn't sure what to do. Before either bride set her wedding date, Dinah answered "yes" to each of their bridesmaid requests. But when she discovered soon after that both weddings would be on the same day—and in different cities—she was stumped.

What was proper etiquette? And how could she possibly choose, without offending one of the brides forever? She prided herself on being a good friend and doing the right thing, so this situation was especially difficult.

So she simply flipped a coin to decide, and called the unlucky party. She explained the situation honestly—and with plenty of time in advance—so the bride had no choice but to understand. It was an unfortunate dilemma, and the bride knew there was nothing the bridesmaid could do about it. So instead of being offended, the bride considered herself lucky that the bridesmaid could still come to her shower and bachelorette party, which didn't conflict with anything.

ALERT!

When scheduling vacations or inflexible social engagements, don't forget to check with the bride first, so you won't conflict with the wedding or any vital wedding preparties.

The moral? Do the best you can. Be straightforward and honest with the bride about any potential problems, and you won't cause any long-term hard feelings. Even if you can't fulfill your role as bridesmaid, you can still be there for the bride in other ways, before and/or after the wedding.

The Unavoidable Illness

In Chicago one sunny Saturday in May, preparations were well underway for a beautiful wedding at one of the city's finer locales. Less than two miles away, one of the bridesmaids had awoken with a nasty stomach flu, apropos of nothing–she hadn't been drinking the night before, she had avoided strange foods, she wasn't pregnant–she had simply succumbed to a bad bug at a most unfortunate time.

After her fifth trip to the powder room in an hour, she was so weak and feverish she couldn't imagine leaving her bed, much less walking up the aisle in front of hundreds of people. Not to mention that she didn't trust herself more than ten feet from a bathroom.

So she called the bride and broke the news. The bride was of course disappointed, but she realized how horrible the bridesmaid felt–both physically and because she felt so guilty about missing the wedding. So the bride decided the wedding would have to come to the bridesmaid–at least for a moment or two. On their way from the bride's home to the ceremony, they had their limo stop at the bridesmaid's apartment to deliver chicken soup and ginger ale. And during the ceremony, one of the other bridesmaids put her cell phone speaker on, so that the sick bridesmaid could hear the bride and groom exchange vows.

The moral? There's nothing you can do about getting sick. And if you've got a selfless and thoughtful bride like this one, you can still be a part of the festivities.

ESSENTIAL

Take good care of yourself the week before the wedding, so you don't get sick or feel run-down. Get plenty of sleep, avoid other sick people (if possible), and try not to take on too much stressful activity.

Acts of God

Sometimes events happen that are way beyond the predictable: a terrible snowstorm, a city-wide power outage, or an act of war. They're bad enough when you're going through the motions of day-to-day life. But when they interrupt months of planning and expectations surrounding a wedding, they're even tougher to handle. The following are some real stories of brides and bridesmaids and how they overcame some circumstances truly beyond their control.

September 11 Fallout

The weekend after September 11, many brides considered canceling their weddings, or scaling them back considerably. Not only was the entire country still in shock, but nationwide transportation had been at a standstill for almost three days. These feelings seemed to hit brides on the East Coast especially hard, particularly in New York City. Many families were struggling with the idea of celebrating so soon after all the suffering.

One Boston bride, after much consideration, decided to go ahead with the wedding as planned. She and her family called all the out-of-town guests to let them know the wedding would go on, but that the bride and groom would surely understand if they couldn't make it to town. In those uncertain first few days after the attacks, the bride didn't want to make anyone feel as if they had to fly if they didn't feel comfortable with it, or even to leave home and family if they didn't want to.

FACT

As a bridesmaid, a little extra effort can go a long way. This might mean giving a wedding guest a ride to the airport, cat-sitting for the bride while she's on her honeymoon, or creating a "Welcome Home" sign to greet the newlyweds upon their return.

One of her bridesmaids was living in Australia at the time. Her flight was scheduled to arrive in Boston two days before the wedding—Thursday, September 13. But because of all the flight cancellations, delays, and traveler backups at airports across the country, it became very clear, very quickly that the Los Angeles airport—where she had arrived with relative ease via a flight from Australia—was about as far as she could expect to fly that weekend. But she was not content to miss this wedding. So she and her boyfriend rented a car and drove through to Boston from L.A., making it just in time for the wedding—a little tired, but no less excited to be there. In fact, most of the out-of-town wedding guests ended up attending one way or another.

Most guests felt absolutely compelled to go, in fact. Celebrating life and happiness seemed more important than ever, in the face of so much death and uncertainty. The wedding was very emotional, and the bride couldn't have appreciated the efforts of this bridesmaid—and the rest of her guests—anymore.

The moral? Never underestimate the love of good friends and family.

Stormy Weather

The timing was awful. Weather forecasters had been predicting nasty weather throughout the week, but no one expected a full-blown hurricane to be blowing up the eastern coastline. So no one was too worried until the morning of the wedding, when the actual hurricane hit.

One bridesmaid was traveling from New York City to a wedding in the suburbs, normally a quick, easy commute. She had planned to take a train that would get her to the hotel in more than enough time to shower, get dressed, and pose for prewedding pictures. Unfortunately, the force of the wind and rain affected the train's progress, which traveled at a maximum speed of ten miles an hour—when it was traveling at all. For three hours (normally a half-hour trip), the train started and stopped, started and stopped.

The bridesmaid grew increasingly panicked, wondering whether she should get off and take a cab, rent a car–anything to get her there in time for her cousin's wedding. Finally the train arrived at its destination. The bridesmaid raced to the hotel, threw on her dress in her grandmother's hotel room, and raced to the lobby for pictures, which were already well underway. Needless to say, the bride was none too pleased by her very late arrival.

The moral? Take precautions against acts of God. Don't rely on public transportation. If you can, sleep as close to the wedding site as you can get. After all, you never know when the odd hurricane will spring up.

Girls Will Be Girls

At times, we are our own worst enemies. Whereas guys can virtually ignore each other, verbally abuse each other, and even get in fistfights and remain best friends, girls make it a bit more difficult on each other. Failing to return a phone call can become a major offense. Neglecting to show up to a promised event can be a total deal-breaker. And then there are the more subtle transgressions, like not being excited enough when a friend reports good news, or those sly put-downs that only a friend could recognize. These are the things that only a woman would notice, or really care about.

Unfortunately, these kinds of subtle offenses can become monumental when they surround a wedding. Possibly it's because they're infused with so many expectations and so much symbolism. There are some women who keep a mental tally of their "bridesmaid list" throughout their lives, as a way of defining their ongoing relationships with other women. This list inevitably changes from the teen years until the day she gets married, but it never loses its significance–a declaration to the world of the women the bride considers her favorite people, her best friends.

That's why being asked to be a bridesmaid can be such an honor–and not being asked can be so hurtful. It's also why failure to live up to one's bridesmaid duties can be so offensive. The bride feels she's put her public trust in you. If you should fail to live up to it, it's proof that you don't care much about her or your relationship.

It's complicated being a woman. That's why the following stories have been included. They all have one thing in common–they'd probably never happen to a man.

The High-Maintenance Monster

Unfortunately, you can be a perfect bridesmaid and still be abused. Take the case of the Salt Lake City bridesmaid. The bride was a friend of hers from childhood, and though they weren't as close as they once had been, they still managed to keep in touch even though they lived in different cities (San Diego, for the bride).

The bridesmaid had done everything she was supposed to. She helped plan a shower from afar, attended the shower and the bachelorette party in San Diego, ordered her dress on time, and e-mailed or called the bride at least once a week to provide a little moral support.

But for this high-maintenance bride, nothing would have been good enough. She was offended that the bridesmaid hadn't attended two additional showers that had been thrown for her in San Diego–she couldn't make those, but she had even been careful to send gifts in her stead–and she was upset that the bridesmaid couldn't come to town a few days before the wedding to help with last-minute details. Because of a demanding work schedule, the bridesmaid, despite her best intentions, simply couldn't take the time off.

FACT

As a bridesmaid, it's your duty to attend all prewedding parties. However, if they're all out of town, there's an exception to the rule. If you can't attend all of them, talk to the bride to see whether she'd prefer you at any one or two specific events.

At the rehearsal and during the wedding day preparations, the bridesmaid dealt with the bride's far-from-warm reception. In fact, the bride pretty much ignored her while showering attention and praise on the other bridesmaids. So the bridesmaid made up her mind that she would serve out her duties with dignity, and ditch the friendship for good. This wasn't the first time she had dealt with passive-aggressive behavior from the bride, and she decided she wouldn't take it any longer.

The moral? You don't have to be a doormat. While you should fulfill your bridesmaid duties and try to go beyond them in the name of friendship, you can only do your best. If the bride resents that, it may be time to re-evaluate the friendship.

The Bridesmaid Who Never Was

Sometimes being asked to be a bridesmaid can be a dreaded obligation; the cost, the travel, and the effort may seem burdensome. Even so, *not* being asked can be an even worse blow. After all, if you're not asked to be a friend's bridesmaid—and you were totally expecting it—it can throw your entire sense of perception into a tailspin. Does this person not value me? Have I done something to offend her? Have I been living in a dream world, believing we were much closer than we are? These are some of the questions you may be faced with when snubbed from bridesmaid duty.

Then there are those friendships that you recognize have been on the rocks. You hope you'll be asked to be a bridesmaid nonetheless, as a good faith gesture toward reconciliation. Or for old times' sake. Or simply because the rest of your group of friends will be bridesmaids, and you don't want to miss out on the fun.

On top of all that, to be publicly rejected is embarrassing. No matter what the reasons, being overlooked as a bridesmaid can bring back those awful, primal grade-school feelings again, like when your fifth-grade best friend suddenly found a new one.

How should you deal with this? One Washington, D.C., non-bridesmaid, stung that she wasn't asked to be a part of her college girlfriend's wedding party, decided to shun the wedding completely. She felt especially hurt, because the bride had been a bridesmaid in her wedding just two years before. The reasons she was ignored are as layered as a wedding cake—years of perceived wrongs against each other had resulted in hard feelings and a lack of communication, and they'd simply drifted apart without ever hashing out their problems.

ALERT!

If you haven't been asked to be a bridesmaid—and you have other friends who have—try not to put them in the middle of the situation. While it may be tempting to solicit their allegiance, they're also trying to be sincere participants in the upcoming nuptials.

While they still ran into each other at the social functions of mutual friends, there was definitely some long-term resentment that had built. For the non-bridesmaid, not being asked was the last straw in an already tenuous friendship. She decided that she'd be uncomfortable attending the prewedding events and the wedding itself–so she didn't.

Then there was the bride in Memphis who was having a small, simple wedding with just three bridesmaids–two sisters and a cousin. A close friend of hers from college couldn't believe she wasn't asked to participate in the wedding. In fact, she confronted the bride about it. In this case, it was a smart idea. The bride was then able to explain that she wanted to keep her wedding low-key and that she didn't want to burden her friends with the obligations of buying a dress, throwing a shower, and so on.

Her friend was then able to understand that not being asked wasn't meant as a personal slight. Rather, it was a personal decision about how the bride wished to style her wedding. For this bride, choosing bridesmaids didn't symbolize who was in the in-crowd versus who was out.

The moral? If you're feeling hurt about being excluded from a friend's wedding party, and the friendship is worth it to you, talk to the offending bride. If it's the last straw in an already declining friendship, it may simply be time to cut your losses. It could also be a clue to treat this relationship in accordance–as a more casual friendship or acquaintance.

The Drama Queen

We all know the type. It's amazing, in fact, how the tilt of the earth's axis is so tied to her every move. No matter what the occasion, it's all about her. No matter what anyone's problem, she's got one to top it. And no matter how funny the story, she's got one that's funnier. And while she may be irritating, she can also be a good friend. That's the reason one New York City bride chose just the type to be one of her bridesmaids (we'll call her Lucy), despite some of her selfish habits.

Of course, the bride, Alex, should have expected that not everything would go smoothly. During the engagement, Lucy first had a messy breakup with her boyfriend. And in a dramatic scene she described to anyone who'd listen in great detail, she also quit her job—she threw a glass of water in her boss's face, to be precise. At every prewedding event, the party quickly seemed to become less about celebrating the bride and more about attending to the bridesmaid. Because of her innate self-involvement, Lucy never even noticed she was stealing the spotlight from Alex with her myriad dramas, stories, and complaints.

ESSENTIAL

Try not to demand too much attention at the wedding or prewedding events. It's the bride's turn to bask in the spotlight. She shouldn't have to share it, for better or worse, with you.

The last straw for the bride came on her wedding day, when she was informed during the photo session that Lucy had disappeared. She tried not to sweat it and went on to take pictures without her . . . .until she found out later that Lucy been caught with an ex-boyfriend in a compromising position in one of the back rooms. The worst part was that the ex-boyfriend had since gotten married–and his wife was a guest at the wedding, too. Of course, the scandal became the talk of the wedding, and the joy of the wedding, unfortunately, became almost secondary.

The moral? Behave. Try not to steal the spotlight from the bride at any wedding-related events. This means saving big announcements for a more suitable time and behaving like a respectable person. Let someone else bask in the attention for once.

A Family Affair

There's nothing like family to get in the way of happiness. (Kidding.) But even in the most harmonious of families, some sticky situations can arise while planning and hosting a wedding.

So when it comes to mixing bridesmaid and family issues, it's best to err on the side of caution. This is true for circumstances ranging from deciding whether or not to accept a bridesmaid post from your future sister-in-law to dealing with being the unmarried maid of honor for your little sister. The following stories illustrate some difficult family affairs bridesmaids have faced and how they got through them fully intact.

Touchy Situation

When Deirdre from Philadelphia was asked to be in her friend Susan's wedding, she was a bit surprised. Though the two had been friends since childhood, Susan had formerly dated Deirdre's brother for about three years. They remained friends after the breakup, but Deirdre was still surprised that Susan would want her to play such a large part in her big day, especially when it meant she was marrying another guy.

But Susan wouldn't dream of getting married without her childhood friend Deirdre playing a part. After all, they'd been friends long before Susan dated her brother; why should that change anything now? Unfortunately, Deirdre's brother didn't see it that way—he was angry when Deirdre told him she'd be taking part in Susan's wedding.

Though Susan had moved on from their relationship, he hadn't—and he was offended that his own sister would "condone" Susan's marriage to another man. Unfortunately, everyone except Deidre's brother knew the relationship was long over, and that's why Deirdre felt okay saying "yes" to Susan's bridesmaid request in the first place.

But after her brother's reaction, Deirdre didn't know what to do. Should she pull out of the proceedings? Should she honor her commitment to Susan? She felt torn between her family, her friend, and her word.

Fortunately, Deirdre's mother intervened. She had a sit-down with Deirdre's brother, explaining that because Deirdre had given her promise, and because she was still good friends with Susan, she could only continue to honor her commitment as bridesmaid. And just because things didn't work out for him and Susan, it wasn't fair to expect that Deirdre would end her relationship with her, too.

So Deirdre remained a bridesmaid. It may have been the best thing that could have happened for her brother. He finally came to realize that the relationship was over and that it was time to move on. Like a fairy-tale ending, he had even met someone else by the time his ex was boarding the plane to her honeymoon.

The moral? When being a bridesmaid threatens to compromise certain allegiances, take diplomatic action rather than ignoring the situation.

Ignored

When Jill's younger brother got engaged, she couldn't have been happier. She had heard his fiancée was a lovely person, though she'd never met her. The two lived across the country from Jill, and had been dating for less than a year. As the engagement period went on, she waited for the phone call asking her to be bridesmaid—Jill had included all *her* husband's sisters in her own wedding, after all. So she never even questioned the fact that her brother's new gal would, too.

But as time went on, and the phone didn't ring, Jill realized that a request may not be forthcoming. She asked her mother, who hadn't yet heard about the bride's final picks for the wedding party. Finally, she questioned her brother. Her brother informed her that the bride, Sarah, had asked her two sisters and her best friend, for a total of three bridesmaids. They didn't want to go overboard with the size of their wedding party, he said. And because they'd never met, Sarah didn't feel comfortable asking Jill. In fact, she'd assumed that Jill wouldn't want to bother with the dress and all the duties that go with being bridesmaid, especially because Jill had two young children.

But Jill was very offended. In her world, this wasn't how things were done–future in-laws were always included in the wedding party. She felt snubbed before she even met Sarah and decided she probably wasn't going to like her. Her mother didn't help matters, and was equally outraged that Jill wouldn't be included in the wedding party. When they finally all came together for the couple's engagement party a month later, the situation was definitely tense. Jill didn't extend Sarah a very warm welcome to the family, and it made Sarah feel sad and uncomfortable.

Sarah wasn't sure how to proceed. She knew Jill was offended she wasn't asked to be in the wedding party, and though Sarah felt she was acting immaturely–they had never even met, after all–this was her future sister-in-law, and she'd have to deal with her for a long time. To salve the bruised egos, Sarah went ahead and asked Jill to take part in the wedding. And though it seemed to Sarah that this gesture might be too little, too late, Jill was pleased as punch. She fully embraced Sarah after that, and all in the family was harmonious again.

The moral? Don't extrapolate your behavior onto everyone else. Just because you would ask your ten best friends and three coworkers to take part in your wedding doesn't mean everyone else would, too. If you haven't been asked to be a bridesmaid, try to put yourself in the bride's shoes before becoming paranoid and/or taking it personally. And if you still feel it's an unjustified snub, try to get to the bottom of the situation.

Always a Bridesmaid

When Laura's little sister, Bridget, got engaged, she couldn't have been happier for her. She knew that Bridget had found a great guy and that they were totally compatible. But while Laura was happy for Bridget, she wasn't feeling very happy about herself—five years Bridget's senior, she wasn't even dating anyone at the time. Unfortunately, the engagement was bringing her insecurities and loneliness into sharp perspective—Laura felt just miserable. And on top of that, she felt guilty that she felt miserable. Why couldn't she just feel happy for her sister?

Things didn't get better as the engagement progressed. At Bridget's shower, she was on the receiving end of insensitive questions from some of the older relatives: "Well, what about you, Laura? When are you getting married?" As if it wasn't bad enough dealing with being single with no current prospects, now she had to deal with it publicly. And of course, she'd be attending the wedding dateless. She imagined her whole family hitting the dance floor with their significant others, while she sat at a table, nursing her drink, all alone.

Nothing could have actually been farther from reality–she was so busy greeting family and friends, and helping Bridget, that she wouldn't have had time for a date, anyway. And she even ended up meeting someone at the wedding–one's of the groom's old friends from college, who'd come into town for the wedding. They dated long-distance after that, and though things ultimately didn't work out, it was just the boost Laura needed–she met her future fiancé soon after. It just goes to show that you don't *always* have to be the bridesmaid.

QUESTION?

I don't have a boyfriend right now. Should I bring a random date to the wedding?
Probably not. Because you'll be so busy, and he presumably won't know anyone, you may end up feeling obliged to entertain him, which could distract you from your bridesmaid duties, or your own good time. Go solo, and have fun.

The moral? Things don't always work out on a timeline of our choosing. If you're feeling down about being single while your friend or family member is blissfully engaged, remember that your day will eventually come, too. And try, hard as it may be, to bask in the residual joy of the bride's happiness.

Appendix

Worksheets

Bridal Party Who's Who

Maid of Honor
Name: ____________________
____
Address: ____________________
____
____
Telephone: ____________________
E-mail: ____________________

Matron of Honor
Name: ____________________
____
Address: ____________________
____
____
Telephone: ____________________
E-mail: ____________________

Bridesmaid
Name: ____________________
____
Address: ____________________
____
Telephone: ____________________
E-mail: ____________________

Bridesmaid
Name: ____________________
____
Address: ____________________
____
____
Telephone: ____________________
E-mail: ____________________

Bridesmaid
Name: ____________________
____
Address: ____________________
____
____
Telephone: ____________________
E-mail: ____________________

Bridesmaid
Name: ____________________
____
Address: ____________________
____
Telephone: ____________________
E-mail: ____________________

Bridesmaid

Name: ______________________

____

Address: ______________________

____

____

Telephone: ______________________

E-mail: ______________________

Bridesmaid

Name: ______________________

____

Address: ______________________

____

____

Telephone: ______________________

E-mail: ______________________

Bridesmaid

Name: ______________________

____

Address: ______________________

____

____

Telephone: ______________________

E-mail: ______________________

Bridesmaid

Name: ______________________

____

Address: ______________________

____

____

Telephone: ______________________

E-mail: ______________________

Flower Girl

Name: ______________________

____

Address: ______________________

____

____

Telephone: ______________________

E-mail: ______________________

Other Honor Attendants:

Name: ______________________

____

Address: ______________________

____

____

Telephone: ______________________

E-mail: ______________________

Bridesmaids' Attire

Store Where Purchased:

Address: ______________________________

Telephone: ______________________________

Store hours: ______________________________

Directions: ______________________________

Salesperson: ______________________________

Description of Dress

Manufacturer: ______________________________

Style number: ______________________________

Color: ______________________________

Dress size: ______________________________

Total cost of dress: ______________________________

Deposit paid: ______________________________

Balance due: ______________________________

Delivery date: ______________________________

Fitting date #1: ______________ Time: ______________

Fitting date #2: ______________ Time: ______________

Fitting date #3: ______________ Time: ______________

Cost of alterations: ______________________________

Description of Shoes

Store where purchased: ______________________________

Manufacturer: ______________________________

Style number: ______________________________

Size: ______________________________

Color: ______________________________

Description of Accessories

Gloves: ______________________________

Store where purchased: ______________________________

Hosiery: ______________________________

Store where purchased: ______________________________

Jewelry: ______________________________

Store where purchased: ______________________________

Important Dates

Use this to keep track of the important dates that are related to wedding events.

Wedding date: ______________________________

____

Rehearsal dinner: ______________________________

____

Bridesmaids' luncheon: ______________________________

____

Bridesmaid's shower: ______________________________

____

Other shower: ______________________________

____

Bachelorette party: ______________________________

____

Bachelor party: ______________________________

____

Engagement party: ______________________________

____

Shower Guest List

Name: ____________________
Address: __________________
Telephone: ________________
RSVP ❐

Name: ____________________
Address: __________________
Telephone: ________________
RSVP ❐

Name: ____________________
Address: __________________
Telephone: ________________
RSVP ❐

Name: ____________________
Address: __________________
Telephone: ________________
RSVP ❐

Name: ____________________
Address: __________________
Telephone: ________________
RSVP ❐

Name: ____________________
Address: __________________
Telephone: ________________
RSVP ❐

Name: ____________________
Address: __________________
Telephone: ________________
RSVP ❐

Name: ____________________
Address: __________________
Telephone: ________________
RSVP ❐

Name: ____________________
Address: __________________
Telephone: ________________
RSVP ❐

Name: ____________________
Address: __________________
Telephone: ________________
RSVP ❐

Name: ____________________
Address: __________________
Telephone: ________________
RSVP ❐

Name: ____________________
Address: __________________
Telephone: ________________
RSVP ❐

Shower Planning Checklist

Three (or more) months before:

- ❒ Decide on type of shower
- ❒ Decide on time of day
- ❒ Choose a location
- ❒ Set a date
- ❒ Set a budget
- ❒ Compile guest list
- ❒ Select caterer
- ❒ Select florist
- ❒ Shop for and order party favors
- ❒ Reserve space for shower (if applicable)

Six weeks before:

- ❒ Confirm time and date with caterer
- ❒ Confirm time and date with florist
- ❒ Send out invitations

Five weeks before:

- ❒ Begin recording guest responses

Four weeks before:

- ❒ Finalize details with caterer
- ❒ Finalize details with florist
- ❒ Purchase shower gift for bride

One week before:

- ❒ Finalize number of guests with caterer OR
- ❒ Shop for liquor and nonperishables (if throwing shower yourself)
- ❒ Plan seating arrangements
- ❒ Pick up and arrange shower favors

A few days before:

- ❒ Begin preparing food

Shower Budget

Item	*Description*	*Projected Cost*	*Actual Cost*	*Balance Due*
Space rental	________	________	________	________
Caterer	________	________	________	________
Food and liquor costs (if throwing at home)	________	________	________	________
Flowers/decorations	________	________	________	________
Shower favors	________	________	________	________
Prizes for shower games	________	________	________	________
Shower gift	________	________	________	________

Shower Gift List

Description of gift	*Gift-giver's name*	*Thank-you note sent*

Bachelorette Party Guest List

Name: ________________
Address: ______________
Telephone: ____________
RSVP ❒

Name: ________________
Address: ______________
Telephone: ____________
RSVP ❒

Name: ________________
Address: ______________
Telephone: ____________
RSVP ❒

Name: ________________
Address: ______________
Telephone: ____________
RSVP ❒

Name: ________________
Address: ______________
Telephone: ____________
RSVP ❒

Name: ________________
Address: ______________
Telephone: ____________
RSVP ❒

Name: ________________
Address: ______________
Telephone: ____________
RSVP ❒

Name: ________________
Address: ______________
Telephone: ____________
RSVP ❒

Name: ________________
Address: ______________
Telephone: ____________
RSVP ❒

Name: ________________
Address: ______________
Telephone: ____________
RSVP ❒

Name: ________________
Address: ______________
Telephone: ____________
RSVP ❒

Name: ________________
Address: ______________
Telephone: ____________
RSVP ❒

Bachelorette Party Checklist

Three (or more) months before:

- ❒ Decide on type of bachelorette party
- ❒ Decide on time of day
- ❒ Choose a location
- ❒ Set a date
- ❒ Set a budget
- ❒ Compile guest list
- ❒ Begin pricing transportation options, such as limos
- ❒ Begin shopping for party props (especially if ordering online)

Six weeks before:

- ❒ Make reservations at a restaurant or club, if applicable
- ❒ Order and put deposit down on transportation or limousine service
- ❒ Order and put deposit down on "entertainment"
- ❒ Send out invitations or begin getting the word out via e-mail or phone

Four weeks before:

- ❒ Make final bachelorette goody and game purchases

One week before:

- ❒ Confirm limo and entertainment services
- ❒ Shop for liquor and nonperishables (if throwing party yourself)
- ❒ Send out e-mail reminder to all those attending

A few days before:

- ❒ Shop for perishable items
- ❒ Make any food you can ahead of time
- ❒ Clean your house

Bachelorette Party Budget

Item	*Description*	*Projected Cost*	*Actual Cost*	*Balance Due*
Limo or transportation rental				
Dinner				
Food and liquor costs (if throwing party at home)				
Decorations/ bachelorette props				
Stripper				
Games and prizes				
Gift for bride				

Index